MW00651412

History of Wyoming

A Captivating Guide to Historical Events and Facts You Should Know About the Cowboy State

© Copyright 2023 - All rights reserved.

The content contained within this book may not be reproduced, duplicated, or transmitted without direct written permission from the author or the publisher.

Under no circumstances will any blame or legal responsibility be held against the publisher, or author, for any damages, reparation, or monetary loss due to the information contained within this book, either directly or indirectly.

Legal Notice:

This book is copyright protected. It is only for personal use. You cannot amend, distribute, sell, use, quote, or paraphrase any part, or the content within this book, without the consent of the author or publisher.

Disclaimer Notice:

Please note the information contained within this document is for educational and entertainment purposes only. All effort has been executed to present accurate, up-to-date, reliable, and complete information. No warranties of any kind are declared or implied. Readers acknowledge that the author is not engaging in the rendering of legal, financial, medical, or professional advice. The content within this book has been derived from various sources. Please consult a licensed professional before attempting any techniques outlined in this book.

By reading this document, the reader agrees that under no circumstances is the author responsible for any losses, direct or indirect, that are incurred as a result of the use of the information contained within this document, including, but not limited to, errors, omissions, or inaccuracies.

Free Bonus from Captivating History (Available for a Limited time)

Hi History Lovers!

Now you have a chance to join our exclusive history list so you can get your first history ebook for free as well as discounts and a potential to get more history books for free! Simply visit the link below to join.

Captivatinghistory.com/ebook

Also, make sure to follow us on Facebook, Twitter and Youtube by searching for Captivating History.

Table of Contents

INTRODUCTION 1

CHAPTER 1 - PREHISTORY AND NATIVE INHABITANTS 3

CHAPTER 2 - EXPLORATION AND FUR TRADE ERA (1700S - 1800S) 11

CHAPTER 3 - WESTWARD EXPANSION AND THE OREGON TRAIL
(1800S) 18

CHAPTER 4 - TERRITORIAL WYOMING (1800S) 33

CHAPTER 5 - THE WYOMING CATTLE BOOM AND JOHNSON
COUNTY WAR (LATE 1800S) 43

CHAPTER 6 - WOMEN'S SUFFRAGE IN WYOMING (LATE 1800S) 54

CHAPTER 7 - WYOMING BECOMES A STATE (1890) 65

CHAPTER 8 - THE ENERGY FRONTIER 69

CHAPTER 9 - MODERN WYOMING (LATE 20TH CENTURY
TO PRESENT) 78

CHAPTER 10 - WYOMING'S NATURAL BEAUTY AND
CONSERVATION EFFORTS 84

CONCLUSION 89

HERE'S ANOTHER BOOK BY CAPTIVATING HISTORY THAT YOU
MIGHT LIKE.. 91

FREE BONUS FROM CAPTIVATING HISTORY (AVAILABLE FOR A
LIMITED TIME).. 92

REFERENCES 93

Introduction

Wyoming, often overlooked amidst its more densely populated counterparts, possesses a narrative that is both distinctive and compelling. Our journey through the pages of Wyoming's history begins here, where we endeavor to establish context, articulate purpose, and chart our path through time.

In the heart of the American West, Wyoming's geography serves as both a backdrop and protagonist in its history. The state's topography is as varied as its past, with expansive plains yielding to formidable mountain ranges, including the towering Rocky Mountains dominating the western skyline. To the east, the sprawling plains of Wyoming stretch out, a stark contrast to the mountainous beauty of the west. The state boasts expansive deserts, clear lakes, winding rivers, and the remarkable geothermal features of Yellowstone National Park, all markers of the powerful natural forces at work here.

This varied geography has deeply influenced Wyoming's history. Rich in resources like coal, oil, and natural gas, the state drew settlers and businesspeople alike. Their efforts and industries have significantly shaped Wyoming's economy and environment. Moreover, Wyoming's strategic location, brimming with historic trails and railways, rendered it an important waypoint for pioneers and traders during the era of westward expansion.

The significance of Wyoming's history extends beyond its own borders. Though Wyoming has one of the smallest populations in the US, its impact on the country's growth is notable. From its beginnings with the fur trade in its wild landscapes to its leading role in women's suffrage, earning it the title "The Equality State," Wyoming has been a hub for significant social, political, and economic changes.

Indeed, Wyoming's history encapsulates the quintessential American experience—a narrative of encounters and exchanges between indigenous cultures and European explorers, struggles for territorial and statehood status, and the waxing and waning of industries that mirrored the nation's broader trends. Its stories of fortitude in the face of adversity—whether battling inclement winters, navigating economic downturns, or confronting environmental challenges—resonate harmoniously with the broader American saga.

Within these pages, we endeavor to offer a comprehensive and accessible account of Wyoming's history. Our exploration will encompass not only the pivotal events and prominent figures but also the subtler sociocultural and environmental factors that have lastingly molded the state. We will delve into the narratives of Native American tribes, stewards of this land for millennia, the enterprising fur trappers who ventured through Wyoming's rugged terrain in pursuit of prosperity, pioneers who embarked on the perilous Oregon Trail, suffragettes who ignited the path toward women's rights, and industrialists who harnessed Wyoming's natural resources.

Our expedition through time will not conclude with the past; we will also consider Wyoming's contemporary challenges and opportunities. These include the delicate equilibrium between economic development and environmental preservation, shifting demographic landscape, evolving political dynamics, and the state's role in national energy production.

Join us as we navigate this complex historical tapestry, unraveling the intricate threads that weave together the story of Wyoming—a tale both enduring and ever-evolving, reflective of the remarkable individuals and forces that have molded this great state.

Chapter 1 – Prehistory and Native Inhabitants

In Wyoming's vast expanse, our story begins in a time that stretches back thousands of years. This chapter takes us on a journey to ancient Wyoming, where the landscape was quite different and the people who lived there were resourceful and tough. This time began with the Paleo-Indian period, setting the stage for a complex history. We'll explore the lives of the state's earliest inhabitants, who were nomadic hunters and gatherers crafting simple yet effective stone tools. Here lay the beginning of human history, where people roamed the plains, hunted large game, and adapted to a changing environment. It's a story of survival, connection to the land, and the beginnings of Wyoming's rich history.

The Paleo-Indian Period in Wyoming

The Paleo-Indian period in Wyoming takes us back to a time before recorded history, from about 14,000 to 6,000 BCE. During this era, Wyoming's vast landscape witnessed some of the earliest footsteps of human habitation on the North American continent.

Around 14,000 years ago, the last major ice age waned, gradually leading to a drier and warmer post-glacial environment. As a result, the mammoth, mastodon, camel, short-faced bear, and horse—all adapted to the cooler glacial conditions—disappeared or shrank in size, marking significant ecological changes.

Evidence of humans living in the region now labeled Yellowstone National Park dates to this period. A Clovis point was discovered near

Corwin Springs, about twelve miles north of the park. These points represent the tools used by Paleo-Indian people, and their presence hints at early hunting and survival strategies.

Paleo-Indians were skilled hunters, relying on bison, bighorn sheep, rabbits, deer, and bears for sustenance. While they likely consumed berries and fresh greens, there's limited evidence of plant processing and cooking as part of their diet during this time.

Around 9450 BCE, Paleo-Indians occupied Hell Gap in southeastern Wyoming, creating large spear points without hafting stems ideal for hunting bison—a primary food source for these short-term campers.

By 9330 BCE, Clovis hunters in Wyoming left evidence of the popular hunting technique of herding a mammoth into a bog, where it became trapped. Butchering the animal on site provided a substantial food source for their camps.

Continuing along this chronology, we encounter additional Clovis sites, including the Union Pacific site around 9280 BCE and the Colby site around 9250 BCE. At these locations, Clovis people exhibited their prowess in mammoth hunting and stone tool craftsmanship. Around 9200 BCE, these people were also present at the Sherman site, further highlighting their wide-ranging influence in the region.

Around 8830 BCE, the climate notably changed. In response, the Folsom culture developed. These people crafted smaller, finely-fluted spear points different from the earlier Clovis points. The Folsom people moved slowly across the mountains and into the flatter Great Plains, spanning areas from North Dakota to Mexico, with a firm presence along the Rockies' eastern slopes. Archaeologists have uncovered a camp belonging to this culture on the floodplain of an arroyo in Agate Basin. There, they trapped, killed, and butchered buffalo, using their ribs as the pegs for their hide-covered tents.

By 8750 BCE, Folsom people had moved into the northern Bighorn Basin, residing in circular structures with sand-covered lodge floors. By 7950 BCE, people using Folsom tools extended their influence to the Rattlesnake Pass site, expanding our understanding of their cultural presence.

Lastly, we have the Cody complex. Despite being attributed to the Northern Great Plains around 8500 BCE, these peoples moved their camps into the Rocky Mountains to be closer to the stone they used for tools. In the winter, they moved to lower elevations to better hunt bears, bighorn sheep, deer, and rabbits. Evidence of Cody complex tool users dating to around 7076 BCE was found at the Horner site, which served as a buffalo butchering area, utilizing a corral near the river's edge during fall hunts.

Archaic Period

Between 8,000 and 2,000 years ago, Wyoming entered a period that archaeologists call the Archaic period. The indigenous inhabitants that had traversed the land bridge thousands of years before continued to evolve and adjust to the constantly changing environment and ecological conditions that defined the world as they knew it.

The onset of the Archaic period was marked by significant transformation. Paleo-Indian bison hunting, once the cornerstone of subsistence, notably declined around 9,000 years ago. This shift seems to have been in direct response to the gradual deterioration of the ecological conditions, proving our human ancestors' need for adaptation.

Around 8,000 years ago, the warming climate started to reshape the landscape. The glaciers, once an imposing feature, dwindled to mere remnants high up in the mountains. Concurrently, the stately lodgepole pine fell back into the higher elevations as it was pushed out by more recognizable aspen and Douglas fir varieties. This period witnessed a shift in the diet of prehistoric populations, especially in the mountainous regions of northwest Wyoming. The inhabitants increasingly turned to smaller animals and wild plant foods for subsistence—a dietary transition that coincided with notable changes in the spear point styles that defined the Archaic period.

This period, spanning about 6,500 years in Wyoming, has been segmented into three distinct subperiods according to spear points: Early, Middle, and Late Archaic.

Early Archaic (8,000 to 5,000 years ago)

The Early Archaic period marked the most notable changes, as mentioned. The spear points of the previous Clovis and Paleo-Indian peoples were large with notches on either side of the base of the point—a design still associated with hafting these points into hunting spears. These early communities dwelled in semi-subterranean pit houses. These excavated pits were covered by structures crafted from wood, brush, and hides. Gathering and utilizing plants for various purposes, such as medicine, foods, and manufacturing materials, was a fundamental aspect of life and remained that way for a long time. They harvested wild roots like camas and wild onions using wooden digging sticks; they processed berries, drying and boiling them or mixing them with grease and dried meat to create a portable food now called pemmican, a term used by modern tribes with an oral history that predates their own.

Middle Archaic (5,000 to 3,000 years ago)

Beyond the Early Archaic shift from the Paleo-Indian way of life, most differences are found in the spear point shapes and flaking technology. In the Middle Archaic period, spear design shifted from the notched spearheads of earlier times as subsistence practices adapted to the continuously changing environment. This period was also marked by intensified processing of specific plant foods. Alongside these changes, settlement patterns and sizes suggest the population significantly grew or their nomadic lifestyle increased, with more traveling throughout the landscape. Tipi rings, large circles of stones used to anchor tipi-like structures, began to appear in the archaeological record—a testament to the adaptability and mobility of these newer communities.

Late Archaic (3,000 to 1,500 years ago)

Hafting notches on the sides of stone spearheads shifted to the corners of projectile points, and this became a defining Late Archaic characteristic. Hunting larger mammals and gathering plants continued to be integral to the peoples' survival. The archaeological record is full of large roasting pits identified by the collection of rocks used to heat them.

Plains Woodland Culture

The Plains Woodland culture is an archaeological designation that covers a broad timeframe, ranging from approximately 500 BCE to 900/1000 CE. It's important to note that these dates have regional variations, as the entire era is categorized based on ceramics that are similar to those found in the Eastern Woodland culture in the upper eastern states.

This culture appeared across a vast expanse stretching from present-day Nebraska and Kansas, west of the Missouri River, to the eastern plains of Colorado and Wyoming. A distinctive technological trait of the Plain Woodland culture was the widespread adoption of pottery. This new ceramic tradition showcased remarkable diversity in forms, decorations, and manufacturing practices, underlining the cultural significance.

What truly sets this culture apart is new technologies, most notably pottery and the slow adoption of the bow and arrow. Both marked a significant departure from the preceding Archaic period.

Archaeological excavations have revealed that these communities varied in their house choices. From simple lean-tos to shallow pit houses, these structures varied in construction and complexity. Pit houses had floors and lower walls lined with rock slabs, while post holes hinted at structures made of poles, likely covered with hides and branches. Storage pits and hearths for cooking were also integral components of these homes.

Subsistence strategies still revolved mostly around hunting and gathering. As time passed, the adoption of the bow and arrow instead of spears became clearer, with the use of smaller projectile points. Game like deer, bison, and elk played a vital role in their diet, with smaller animals like rabbits and prairie dogs also providing some food. The Plains Woodland people also harvested animal skins and sinew for crafting clothing and moccasins.

Ground stone milling tools found at archaeological sites support the idea that the people continued to depend on gathering plant materials. These stones were used to process the plants into usable forms. Several sites showed evidence of maize, which became a cornerstone of many Native American diets. This raises the possibility that some of these peoples were practicing minimal agriculture.

Burial practices were diverse. Archaeologists have found individuals interred in pits, crevices in cliffs, or even ossuaries containing disarticulated remains. These burials occasionally included grave goods, providing a glimpse into the material culture and beliefs of these people.

Plains Village Cultures

Overlapping this period of change during the Late Prehistoric in Wyoming, we find other significant cultural shifts on the plains. Spanning roughly from 1000 CE to 1780 CE, the Plains Village culture witnessed the emergence of a more settled way of life that stood in stark contrast to the nomadic traditions of the earlier peoples.

The Plains Village tradition encompasses the archaeological history of the Great Plains, stretching from North Dakota down to Texas, and persisted until the late 18th to mid-19th century (1780/1850 CE). It reveals a remarkable diversity of tribal communities, each with distinct lifestyles and adaptations.

Two overarching classifications among Plains tribes emerged, overlapping to some extent. The first group slowly evolved to a fully nomadic horse culture during the 18th century and followed the American bison herds, though it occasionally practiced agriculture. The tribes of this tradition include the Arapaho, Assiniboine, Blackfoot, Cheyenne, Comanche, Crow, Gros Ventre, Kiowa, Lakota, Lipan, Plains Apache or Kiowa Apache, Plains Cree, Plains Ojibwe, Sarsi, Nakoda, and Tonkawa.

The second branch chose a more sedentary or semi-sedentary lifestyle. These tribes lived in villages, cultivated crops, and engaged in intertribal trade alongside bison hunting. This category comprises the Arikara, Hidatsa, Iowa, Kaw, Kitsau, Mandan, Missouria, Omaha, Osage, Otoe, Pawnee, Ponca, Quapaw, Wichita, and the Santee Dakota, Yanktonai, and Yankton Dakota.

Wyoming was at least a temporary home to many of these nomadic tribes. The Arapaho, Arikara, Bannock, Blackfeet, Cheyenne, Crow, Gros Ventre, Kiowa, Nez Perce, Sheep Eater, Sioux, Shoshone, and Ute tribes have left indelible marks through archaeological sites, petroglyphs, and cultural imprints. The Vore Buffalo Jump in northeast Wyoming, an archaeological site illustrating Plains Indian hunting practices, remains a testament to their rich heritage.

Plains farmers showed remarkable adaptability, developing short-season and drought-resistant crop varieties. They manipulated water resources without relying on irrigation, maximizing the benefits of their limited rainfall. Agricultural pursuits often involved planting crops in the spring, venturing out to hunt bison/buffalo during the summer, and returning to harvest their crops in the fall.

While agricultural practices were pivotal, Plains Village communities continued supplementing their diets through hunting and gathering. The expansive Wyoming landscape, teeming with diverse ecosystems, offered abundant resources the Plains peoples adeptly took advantage of.

We also find a much clearer picture of their rich and diverse cosmologies and worldviews, reflecting distinct and complex spiritual beliefs. Some leaned toward animism and polytheistic elements, while others gravitated toward monotheism or pantheism. Daily life was punctuated by prayer, encompassing individuals and spiritual leaders in solitude and during communal ceremonies like the annual Sun Dance.

Gender roles within the villages were clearly defined and complementary. Women typically owned family homes and most their contents. Their responsibilities encompassed tanning hides, tending crops, gathering wild foods, preparing food, producing clothing, and assembling family homes.

Petroglyphs scattered across Wyoming's landscape provide glimpses into the earliest Native American sites within the state, offering a unique window. Sacred places remain sacred to many tribes.

Devil's Tower

One such example is nestled in northeastern Wyoming: Devil's Tower. This iconic natural wonder has profound cultural significance. For the Plains tribes, Devil's Tower is more than a geological marvel; it is a sacred site often known by distinct names. The Cheyenne refer to it as "Bear's Lodge," "Bear's House," "Bear's Tipi," or "Bear Peak." The Crow simply call it "Bear Lodge." The Lakota have various names for it, such as "Bear Lodge," "Bear Lodge Butte," and "Ghost Mountain." The Kiowa know it as "Aloft on a Rock" and "Tree Rock," with strong astronomical ties. The Arapahoe call it "Bear's Tipi." The Shoshone, while maintaining secrecy about their religious beliefs, also have an association with Devil's Tower.

Devil's Tower by Amaury Michaux
https://www.pexels.com/photo/the-devils-tower-national-monument-in-wyoming-14337686/

Oral histories and sacred narratives have been passed down through generations among these tribes, shedding light on the creation and significance of Devil's Tower. These narratives detail the tower's formation and emphasize its importance to indigenous cultures. For the Arapahoe people, it is the burial place of Drying-Up-Hide.

For the Cheyenne, the tower served as a winter camp and a holy place for worship. Sweet Medicine, a revered figure in their culture, passed away in the vicinity and is also buried at the tower. Sweet Medicine is known for bringing the Four Sacred Arrows to the Cheyenne, which were kept in a secret cave on the tower's south side. His prophecies about the arrival of white settlers and the changes they would bring hold significant historical value.

The Crow used the tower as a place for vision quests. They were known to fast, pray, and build small stone "dream houses" here. These stone structures were around the height of an average man and played a crucial role in their spiritual practices.

Of all the Plains tribes, the Lakota seem to have the most profound connection to Devil's Tower. They considered it sacred and held winter camps there until at least 1816. The tower is an integral part of their creation story, as the Black Hills, including Devil's Tower, is their place of origin. There, they seek spiritual guidance through fasting, prayer, and rituals, such as the Sun Dance, which takes place around the summer solstice. Shamanic healers conducted healing ceremonies at the tower, and oral traditions state that the Great Bear, *Hu Numpa,* imparted sacred language and healing ceremonies at the site. The Lakota also sought out the tower for their vision quests.

Chapter 2 – Exploration and Fur Trade Era (1700s – 1800s)

These indigenous tribes lived unhindered by anything other than neighboring tribes, environmental change, and technological changes through trade for quite some time. Wyoming's vast expanse remained untouched by European influence for centuries after these indigenous peoples had cultivated their rich cultures and traditions. As such, the arrival of European explorers and the dawn of the fur trade brought about countless and dramatic changes.

European Exploration and Mapping

In the mid-18th century, a sense of wonder and adventure beckoned explorers to the wild and untamed landscapes of North America. Among these intrepid souls were the first white folk of European descent known to have reached the lands of Wyoming: Francois and Louis-Joseph, sons of Pierre Gaultier de Varennes, sieur de la Vérendrye. These gentlemen embarked on a historic journey that would etch their names into Wyoming's annals, even with the confusion about whether they stepped foot there.

It was in 1743 that the Verendrye brothers set foot in what sounds like the northeastern corner of Wyoming. Their mission? To uncover a route to the Pacific Ocean, a journey and quest that had troubled explorers for some time. The brothers, of French-Canadian heritage, undertook this perilous expedition as part of their father's grand vision. Pierre Gaultier de Varennes had long dreamed of discovering the elusive

"Western Sea," a dream that had eluded him and countless others.

In 1742, Francois and Louis-Joseph ventured into the heart of the North American continent, making their way to the Mandan villages in west central North Dakota. From there, they journeyed southwest, bringing them face to face with high, wooded mountains. Historians have debated the exact identity of these mountains. Some argue they were the Black Hills of South Dakota, while others suggest they might have been the Big Horn Mountains of northern Wyoming. The ambiguity arises from the generalized nature of their narrative, leaving us to ponder exactly where they were.

Regardless of their route, the brothers retraced their steps back to the Mandans, passing through the mouth of the Bad River near what we now recognize as Pierre, South Dakota. Their journey lasted an arduous eleven months without finding that path to the Pacific, as they found the Rocky Mountains impassable.

The Verendrye brothers' expedition was just the beginning of Wyoming's encounter with European exploration. As we delve deeper into the annals, we will uncover the stories of other intrepid explorers who ventured into this rugged and untamed land.

The Louisiana Purchase of 1803

The year 1803 marked a momentous turning point in Wyoming's history and the broader history of the United States. It was a time when a remarkable event unfolded—the Louisiana Purchase. The acquisition of the Louisiana Territory would alter the landscape of the young nation and lay the foundation for the westward expansion that now defines the American frontier.

Historians often celebrate the Louisiana Purchase as one of the most extraordinary real estate deals in American history, not because of the brilliance of the negotiators but because of the perfect alignment of circumstances. At its inception, the ambition was modest: securing the strategic port of New Orleans and the delta region of the mighty Mississippi River. However, history took an unexpected turn when Napoleon Bonaparte, in dire need of funds for his ambitious military campaigns, made a bold proposition to President Thomas Jefferson. He offered not just New Orleans but the entire Louisiana Territory, an expansive stretch of land that reached far beyond our modern concept of Louisiana, extending beyond the Mississippi River to the imposing Rocky Mountains. Astonishingly, this vast expanse was purchased for a mere $15 million.

While not encompassing all of modern Wyoming, this newly gained territory contained a significant portion of the present-day state. This pivotal transaction, officially ratified by the Senate on October 20, 1803, had far-reaching implications. The United States, in a momentous leap, doubled in size, incorporating territories that would eventually evolve into the states of Louisiana, Arkansas, Missouri, Iowa, Oklahoma, Kansas, Nebraska, North Dakota, South Dakota, and parts of Minnesota, New Mexico, Montana, Wyoming, and Colorado. This deal even extended into small segments of the Canadian provinces of Alberta and Saskatchewan. The Senate's resounding vote of 24 to 7 set the stage for an exciting new chapter in the nation's history.

After the Louisiana Purchase, the federal government started a series of expeditions and surveys. Their mission was clear: explore and map the American West, bringing these vast territories under the jurisdiction of the United States. These determined efforts laid the groundwork for the first reasonably accurate maps of the region, establishing formal boundaries that would significantly impact Wyoming's future.

Fur Trade Companies and Mountain Men

With this land in the expanded United States, vast, uncharted territories held the promise of new frontiers and untold riches. Among the many ventures that sought to capitalize on this potential, none played a more crucial role in shaping Wyoming's history than the fur trade companies and the rugged mountain men who decided to traverse the wilderness.

The remarkable and profitable fur trade in North America peaked in the early 19th century, with Wyoming serving as a vital crossroads. The untamed wilderness of northwestern Wyoming, where the Green, Snake, and Yellowstone rivers originated, was teeming with the perfect wildlife for the demand for fur, notably the prized beaver. The pelts of these flat-tailed creatures were among the most sought-after commodities in a booming, global fur trade, propelling non-indigenous adventurers into the Rocky Mountains in pursuit of fortune.

Wyoming's fur trade era, stretching from the early 1800s to the 1840s, was a period of intense economic activity that shaped the region's early development. The lure of beaver pelts for the fashionable fur hats in demand in Europe and the eastern United States drove trappers, often referred to as mountain men, into the heart of the Rocky

Mountains.

The first fur trade companies to penetrate Wyoming's wilderness recognized the area's potential. Notable among them was the Rocky Mountain Fur Company, founded by William Henry Ashley and Andrew Henry. Ashley's innovative rendezvous system, initiated in 1825, revolutionized the trade. Instead of trappers trekking back to St. Louis each year, the company met them in the field in Wyoming with supplies, creating a bustling, if temporary, fur trade epicenter.

The American Fur Company, under John Jacob Astor, soon entered the scene, setting off a rivalry with the Rocky Mountain Fur Company. Astor's resources allowed for the establishment of a network of trading posts throughout the region, which were more permanent than the rendezvous system. Fort William, later known as Fort Laramie, became one of the most significant posts, a hub for trade with the Northern Plains tribes and a restocking point for trappers heading into the mountains.

Wyoming's fur trade also drew the attention of the Hudson's Bay Company, based in British-controlled Canada. They aimed to create a "fur desert" strategy—overtrapping regions south of the 49th parallel to deplete resources that American companies might otherwise exploit. This competitive trapping, while effective in the short term, eventually contributed to the rapid decline of the beaver population in Wyoming and beyond.

In 1805, François Antoine Larocque made history by trading furs on the banks of the Powder River, marking the region's initial brush with the fur trade. Yet, it was the return of the Lewis and Clark Expedition in 1806 that truly ignited the fever for exploring this area. The expedition's glowing accounts of the abundance of beaver in the mountainous West (Montana) acted like a siren song, luring many brave souls to retrace the steps of these famous explorers.

Among the first to heed the call were John Colter and George Drouillard, former members of the Lewis and Clark Expedition. Employed by Manuel Lisa's St. Louis-based fur trading company, these two men played a vital role in encouraging Indian tribes to trade at a newly established post in 1807, strategically built where the Bighorn and Yellowstone rivers met.

While Lewis and Clark themselves never ventured into the lands that would later become Wyoming, their fellow explorer, John Colter, would leave an indelible mark on what is now Yellowstone. Colter possessed an unparalleled skill set as a hunter and scout. His keen abilities made him an asset to the expedition, and he was often dispatched to hunt game and scout potential trails.

In October 1807, John Colter set out again, alone, on a 500-mile journey despite the cold of winter. Using indigenous people as his experts, he navigated the Wind River Mountains and the Teton Range. Along this route, he was likely the first white man to witness Jackson Hole and Yellowstone Lake. Exploring the region west of modern-day Cody, following the course of the "Stinking Waters" (the Shoshone River). During this time, Colter reported his encounters with geysers and mudpots, eventually earning the area the nickname "Colter's Hell," a part of Yellowstone National Park.

Colter was only the beginning. Trappers soon fanned out across the Wyoming wilderness. One notable figure was Edward Rose, of mixed-race heritage, known for his early presence in the Big Horn Basin around 1809. Rose cultivated friendly relations with the Crow Nation but remains otherwise shrouded in mystery. The historical records didn't deem his work very important.

Reports of Rocky Mountain fur riches soon reached the eastern states, promoting millionaire John Jacob Astor to act. In 1810-11, Astor's Pacific Fur Company started another adventure with Edward Robinson, John Hoback, Jacob Reznor, and, at the lead, the famous Wilson Price Hunt. This journey took them across Wyoming, following the Bighorn/Wind River and crossing the Wind River Mountains through the Union Pass. This path allowed them to capture a glimpse of the majestic Tetons while the Snake River served as their guiding compass.

Until this point, the fur industry relied heavily on trade with Native American tribes for pelts, significantly changing their societies. For instance, firearms, introduced to the Natives through this trade, transformed the dynamics of indigenous communities. Horses, pivotal in warfare, had been crucial in shaping the power balance among tribes. The Shoshone were introduced to horses earlier than many Rocky Mountain tribes, elevating their influence. However, the tide began to turn when smallpox struck the Shoshone in 1781, decimating their population. Concurrently, other tribes, most notably the Blackfeet, acquired firearms from Canadian traders, fundamentally altering the landscape of intertribal dynamics. By the early 1800s, when the fur trade peaked, the once mighty and strong Shoshone had been forced to relocate into the mountains, a move that lost them most of their precious horses. Guns, rapidly traded with various tribes, became a sought-after commodity, underpinning the trade between non-native settlers and indigenous peoples.

Gradually, white trappers took up trapping directly in the field. You can imagine the change in relations this must have caused with Native populations that had begun to depend on this highly sought-after resource for bartering. The fur trade now drew Native Americans and tribes to rendezvous points, fostering a new type of exchange. Trappers and traders offered Euro-American goods, including firearms, metal pots, tobacco, beads, and blankets. Native communities became dependent on these non-native items.

These interactions led to other notable changes: trapper-Native marriages and military alliances. Relations weren't always pleasant, either. Rendezvous points were often the centers for attacks by hostile bands. In 1832, Gros Ventre warriors attacked a supply caravan headed for Green River Valley and another at Pierre's Hole (Teton Valley), Idaho. Trappers joined forces with other native tribes like the Nez Perce and Flathead warriors. This wasn't an unusual occurrence throughout the West, including Wyoming. Colter himself was taken hostage, and his friend was killed. He, surprisingly, was stripped of everything and released.

Everywhere, the fur trade was a melting pot of cultures and ethnicities. In addition to the Native populations residing in Wyoming, members of Eastern tribes contributed significantly to the trapper culture. The Iroquois, Shawnee, and Delaware worked hard alongside white trappers. German, French, Mexican, Scottish, Irish, and other diverse groups further enriched this clash of cultures, making the fur trade a truly global endeavor.

As competition grew fierce, Wyoming saw its first permanent trading post, often referred to historically as a fort. This first was Fort Bonneville, built in 1832 along the upper Green River near present-day Daniel. Alas, this first fort didn't last long, but its sister fort, Fort William on the Laramie River (1834), remained and later became Fort Laramie, eventually becoming a frontier base for the US military. During the same era, more "houses" and forts popped up all over the landscape at strategic points, some becoming indispensable posts for those making the long journey along the Oregon, California, and Mormon trails.

By the late 1830s, fashion had changed, the beaver was nearly trapped out, and the fur trade era in Wyoming began to wane. However, the trails blazed by the mountain men became conduits for westward expansion. Some, like Jim Bridger and Thomas Fitzpatrick, became scouts and guides. Others, like Jedediah Smith, whose explorations had charted much of the West, met untimely ends, their legacies living on in the rugged spirit they imbued in the state.

In fact, many of the trails established by these trappers soon gained traffic. Wagons made themselves known by 1830 at the rendezvous east of the Continental Divide and were eventually guided over the South Pass in 1832 by Benjamin Bonneville. By 1840, which marked the final rendezvous for trappers, wagons heading further west had become a common sight, setting the stage for westward expansion.

Chapter 3 – Westward Expansion and the Oregon Trail (1800s)

The 19th century was a transformative era in the history of the United States marked by considerable westward expansion and the ever-evolving pioneering spirit of the people that made the country their home. Shaping westward expansion were dynamic forces, resilience, and monumental events.

Beginning with the Louisiana Purchase, exploration of the new expanses of land quickly morphed into new settlements and dreams of a better life. With its changing landscapes and abundant natural resources, Wyoming played a pivotal role in this westward expansion thanks to those pioneering fur traders laying the groundwork for future travel. As the United States took its first tentative steps into these uncharted territories, a spirit of curiosity and exploration began to flourish. The region of Wyoming became a crucial corridor for pioneers seeking more fertile lands, economic opportunity, and a fresh start.

The historic Oregon Trail was more than a path through the wilderness that inspired a popular computer game. It was a symbol of hope, ambition, and the unwavering determination of the American people to build a better life for themselves and future generations, including those who would call Wyoming home. From the rugged terrain of the Midwest to the stunning vistas of the Rocky Mountains within Wyoming's borders, from the trials of river crossings to the camaraderie of wagon trains passing through the future state, the Oregon

Trail encapsulated the essence of the American frontier experienced in Wyoming.

The Oregon Trail and Emigration to the West

Spanning over 2,000 miles from the Missouri River to the Pacific Northwest, the Oregon Trail and its companions, the Mormon Pioneer and California trails, carved a central corridor through the heart of Wyoming. These trails were not solitary pathways but a network, like the branches of a tree, creating many variations that eventually established routes on both sides of the main trail. Large rivers such as the Platte, North Platte, Snake, and Columbia often followed alongside the major routes.

As we established earlier, the beginnings of the Oregon Trail can be traced back to the early 19th century when fur traders and trappers explored the vast western territories now owned by the US. From 1811 to 1840, these individuals found the paths, on foot or horseback, that the wagons and settlers would eventually travel. In its early years, the trail was treacherous, limiting passage to those who could navigate its rugged terrain.

However, the 1830s, and particularly 1846 through 1869, marked a significant turning point in travel through this area. An astonishing surge of settlers, farmers, miners, ranchers, business owners, and their families poured onto the trails. Approximately 400,000 individuals, driven by dreams of a brighter future, took this arduous path.

From the perception of the early travelers, the easiest stretch was across the flat, fertile prairies of Nebraska: a 500-mile track through dangerous Indian country. The land gradually grew wilder and more mesmerizing the further they traveled from Independence, Missouri, winding along the Platte River's north fork. This route carried travelers past natural wonders like Chimney Rock and Scotts Bluff, beckoning them into the rugged and wild landscapes of Wyoming near the modern town of Lingle.

Most families started in Iowa, Missouri, or Nebraska Territory, the emigrant routes converging near Fort Kearny, Nebraska Territory, before continuing their westward journey to more fertile farmlands they were told lay beyond the Rocky Mountains. The year 1843 witnessed an epic event, coincidentally called "The Great Migration of 1843" or the "Wagon Train of 1843." It's estimated that between 700 and 1,000 emigrants set out for Oregon in that year alone. Considering the length of the journey and the weather they would want to avoid, most of these travelers would have to leave around the same time. Imagine the site of that many wagons departing across the Great Plains within days or weeks of each other!

For those entering Wyoming on the north bank of the trail, a formidable challenge awaited—fording the deep, swift waters of the North Platte River near Fort Laramie. Fort Laramie, strategically positioned at the meeting of the Laramie and North Platte rivers, became a vital stop on the journey west. Purchased by the U.S. Army in 1848 to safeguard trail travelers, it was the last military outpost before the emigrants reached their destination.

In 1850, a new option emerged for north-side emigrants—loading their wagons onto flatboats, awkwardly pulled across the river by ropes. This daring endeavor came at a steep cost of $1 per wagon, which doesn't seem like much but is equivalent to around $40 today. For many, it was worth the expense to avoid drownings and losing possessions and food, but for others, the price was too steep. Over the years, many ferries materialized at river crossings, significantly increasing the safety and speed of the journey. Although these ferries raised the cost of travel along the trail by around $30 per wagon (equivalent to almost $1200 today), they cut the trip down to between 160 to 170 days by 1843 and even more to between 120 to 140 days by 1860. That's a drastic change from an average of 180 days.

As emigrants ventured deeper into Wyoming, they encountered landmarks made famous today by this trail alongside some challenging terrain. Ten miles northwest of Fort Laramie, the trail led to Sand Point, near present-day Guernsey, Wyoming, an essential campsite and location of the central Star Pony Express station from 1860 to 1861.

Continuing their journey, the wagons formed a single-file line to prepare for their strenuous ascent of the rocky ridges to bypass the marshy lowlands that now sat along the river. The relentless travel of countless hooves and wagon wheels gradually etched a channel into the stone, now immortalized as the Guernsey Ruts or Deep Hill Ruts.

The North Platte provided the almost perfect path into central Wyoming, where they encountered the first large decision point at the Parting of the Ways. Here, they had to choose one of two paths: the Sublette Cutoff or the original route leading southwest toward Fort Bridger and Utah. This stop marked the first in a series of diverging trails, each offering new challenges and rewards.

The Oregon Trail was undeniably dangerous and riddled with physical and emotional challenges. As they approached the Continental Divide, emigrants crossed through landmarks like Devil's Gate, Split Rock, and Ice Slough. While these natural wonders awed the travelers as much as they do us today, they also encountered the barren, wind-swept expanse of Rocky Ridge, another incredibly challenging ascent. Smooth, flat trails and treacherous ascents were punctuated by obstacles, such as alkali waterholes that poisoned livestock and stretches of grassless and waterless land that killed oxen from exhaustion and dehydration. The arid, sagebrush-laden terrain took a toll on the human travelers and their animals, testing their grit and determination.

Even after surpassing the Continental Divide, the challenges persisted as emigrants descended into the breathtaking but perilous Wind River Range. They witnessed the snow-covered peaks as they veered south away from the heart of the mountains.

These are only the opening chapters of their journey along a trail that would define the hopes and aspirations of countless pioneers seeking a new life in the farthest reaches of the American West. Beyond Wyoming, they would encounter new landscapes, cultures, and adversities, forging a path that would become synonymous with the American dream and the resilience of the American people.

Tales from the Trail

Along this perilous journey, countless stories of courage, determination, and the human spirit emerged.

The Donner Party

The Oregon Trail is the backdrop for one of the most haunting stories in American pioneer history: the Donner Party.

In the spring of 1846, an ambitious group of pioneers comprised of families, single men, and hired hands embarked on a journey to California, seeking a better life. George Donner and James Reed, two of the leaders, decided to take a new and supposedly shorter route, the Hastings Cutoff, based on an untested guidebook by Lansford Hastings. This decision, driven by a mix of trust in written accounts and the ambition to expedite their journey, would prove calamitous.

The "shortcut" turned out to be treacherous, leading them through the Wasatch Mountains and the Great Salt Lake Desert, causing significant delays. By the time they reached the Sierra Nevada Mountains, winter had set in earlier than usual. Heavy snowfalls blocked the mountain passes, trapping them with inadequate provisions and shelter.

As days turned into weeks, their food supplies dwindled. Their cattle, essential for food and pulling wagons, were lost or consumed. The harsh conditions, combined with the lack of proper nutrition, led to the death of many, further intensifying the despair and hopelessness that permeated the camp.

By mid-winter, desperation took a dark turn. As the severity of their situation became apparent and with no relief in sight, some members of the party resorted to consuming the remains of their deceased companions to stave off starvation. This grim decision remains the most notorious aspect of their ordeal.

Several relief expeditions were launched from California when word of the stranded party spread. These rescue missions faced their own share of challenges, from harsh weather to navigating the treacherous terrain. Each time a relief group reached the Donner Party, they found fewer survivors and more evidence of the desperate measures the pioneers had resorted to.

Come spring, the ordeal finally ended for the remaining survivors. Of the original eighty-seven members, only forty-eight managed to reach California. The story of their journey, marked by poor decisions, unimaginable hardships, and a fierce will to survive, became a cautionary tale for future pioneers.

Narcissa Whitman

Narcissa Whitman stands as a testament to the determination and courage of women who ventured westward during the 19th century. Along with Eliza Hart Spalding, she was among the first women to journey across the challenging terrain of the Oregon Trail. Their expedition in 1836 was groundbreaking because of not only their gender but also the rich documentation they left behind.

Armed with quills, paper, and an observant eye, Narcissa meticulously detailed her experiences in diaries and letters, painting a vivid picture of life on the trail. Her writings touch on their daily routines, interactions with Native American tribes, the breathtaking landscapes, the trials they faced, and the camaraderie among pioneers. Through her words, the challenges unique to women—from personal safety to maintaining domestic routines in a mobile and often hostile environment—become evident. Her and Spalding's narratives have since become invaluable primary sources, offering historians and readers a window into the female perspective of this significant migration.

With her husband, Dr. Marcus Whitman, Narcissa settled near modern-day Walla Walla, Washington, where they established a mission. Their aim was to convert the local Cayuse people to Christianity. However, cultural misunderstandings and tensions grew, especially after a measles outbreak spread from the mission and decimated the Cayuse, who had no immunity to the disease.

In 1847, these tensions reached a tragic climax in what became known as the Whitman Massacre. Believing the Whitmans were poisoning them, a group of Cayuse attacked the mission, resulting in the deaths of Narcissa, her husband, and twelve others. This event marked a significant turning point in relations between settlers and Native American tribes in the Oregon Territory.

Ezra Meeker

Ezra Meeker's life embodies the pioneering spirit that defines the American West. In 1852, a young Meeker, driven by tales of boundless opportunities in the Pacific Northwest, embarked on the arduous journey across the Oregon Trail. Like many pioneers of his time, he was drawn by the allure of fertile land, economic prospects, and a chance to carve out a new life in the expansive western territories.

Setting out from Iowa with his young family and a wagon train, Meeker encountered the full spectrum of challenges the trail presented: treacherous river crossings, harsh weather, and the ever-present threat of disease. However, through determination and resilience, he successfully navigated these challenges, eventually settling in Washington Territory. There, Meeker thrived, establishing himself as a hop farmer and becoming an influential figure in the community.

Yet, as the decades passed, the Oregon Trail, once bustling with thousands of pioneers, began to fade from national consciousness, overtaken by railroads and modern infrastructure. Recognizing the importance of preserving this crucial chapter of American history, Meeker, in his later years, took it upon himself to retrace his steps.

Starting in 1906, at age seventy-six, Meeker embarked on a journey to retrace the Oregon Trail with the same ox-driven wagon he used over half a century earlier. This expedition, and several more that followed, weren't just acts of nostalgia. They were passionate endeavors to physically mark the trail, erecting monuments and advocating for its preservation. Along the way, he garnered attention from the media, met with presidents, and delivered lectures, ensuring the trail's stories, challenges, and triumphs were not forgotten.

Meeker's tireless efforts culminated in tangible results. His advocacy played a key role in establishing the Oregon Trail as a recognized historical route, ensuring that future generations would understand its significance in shaping the nation.

Ezra Meeker was more than just a traveler of the Oregon Trail; he became its guardian. Even today, his dedication serves as a reminder of the trail's enduring legacy and the importance of preserving the stories that define our shared history.

Native American Conflicts

The Grattan Massacre (1854)

In 1854, near the well-trodden pathways of Fort Laramie, a lost cow unknowingly became the spark of a conflict with lasting consequences. The cow, property of a Mormon traveler, wandered and was killed by High Forehead, a Miniconjou Lakota Sioux. But it wasn't just about a cow; it was about clashing cultures, misunderstood intentions, and the fragile peace of the frontier.

John Grattan, a young lieutenant with more bravado than experience, led a group to address the matter. Instead of seeking understanding or employing patience, Grattan's approach was aggressive, likely because of his lack of knowledge about the Lakota's traditions and values. He met with Chief Conquering Bear, a leader who, ironically, was known for his peacekeeping efforts between the Sioux and the Americans.

What could have been a calm negotiation turned tense. A gunshot—its origin still debated—echoed, changing the day's trajectory. In the chaotic aftermath, Chief Conquering Bear and several of his men were dead. In their grief and anger, the Lakota retaliated, leaving Grattan and his entire party lifeless.

Labeled the Grattan Massacre, the incident wasn't just a tragedy of the moment but a symbol of deeper issues: the constant push and pull between expansion and tradition, settlers and natives. The narrative that spread painted the Sioux as the culprits, which only fueled more conflicts in the years to come.

The Sand Creek Massacre (1864)

The plains and valleys of Wyoming where the Cheyenne once roamed provide a silent backdrop to a haunting episode in US history.

In 1864, the Cheyenne and Arapaho, thinking they were safe near Colorado's Sand Creek because of discussions with the US military, settled in peace. They believed they were under protection because of existing agreements. But Colonel John Chivington and his militia thought differently.

They attacked the encampment suddenly, killing over 230 people, most of whom were women, children, and the elderly. This wasn't a military confrontation; it was a cold-blooded massacre. The horror went beyond the high death toll, with Chivington's men committing unspeakable acts of cruelty.

The Sand Creek Massacre ignited anger and resentment among Native American groups, including those in Wyoming. While it led to national shock and several military investigations, no one, including Chivington, was held accountable.

Red Cloud's War (1866-1868)

The late 1860s saw the Oglala Lakota, led by their formidable chief Red Cloud, in a tug of war with US forces over land that was more than just soil and grass to them—it was home, history, and heritage. The Bozeman Trail, seen by settlers as a convenient route to Montana's goldfields, slashed through the heart of the Lakota's prime hunting lands. As wagons rolled in, they didn't just bring settlers; they brought change, driving away the bison that the Lakota depended on for food, tools, and spiritual ceremonies.

Red Cloud was no passive observer. Seeing the mounting threat, he rallied warriors from across the tribes, using strategy and deep knowledge of the land to mount surprise attacks on US military posts. One such encounter was the Fetterman Fight. What the US troops assumed would be an easy victory turned out to be a carefully laid trap by Red Cloud, showcasing the Lakota's home-ground advantage and tactical prowess.

To ease tensions, the US drafted a new Treaty of Fort Laramie in 1868. This agreement shut down the contentious Bozeman Trail and acknowledged the Black Hills as Lakota territory. It was a promise, a nod to the Lakota's fierce defense of their homeland.

The Flight of the Nez Perce (1877)

The summer of 1877 bore witness to an epic journey. It wasn't a journey of exploration or seeking gold—it was a desperate flight for freedom. The Nez Perce, a tribe that had lived in the Pacific Northwest for centuries, found themselves squeezed by encroaching settlers and the US government's pressures. When orders came to relocate to a small reservation, stripping them of vast swathes of their ancestral lands, many complied. Yet, for a faction of the Nez Perce, the thought of living confined was unbearable.

Under the leadership of Chief Joseph, a group decided to seek refuge in Canada. Their path, filled with hope and despair, meandered through mountains, valleys, and plains, including the rugged terrains of the northwest corner of Wyoming. Pursued relentlessly by the U.S. Army, the Nez Perce showcased their deep understanding of the land, evading capture multiple times. But the relentless pursuit and the challenges of a 1,200-mile trek took its toll.

The Nez Perce's journey, marked by a series of skirmishes and battles, ended just forty miles from the Canadian border. In a heart-wrenching speech, Chief Joseph announced their surrender, uttering the famous words, "I will fight no more forever." It was more than a concession; it was a profound reflection on the trauma, dislocation, and heartbreak that westward expansion brought upon Native American communities.

Important Oregon Trail Locations in Wyoming

This route from Missouri's western edge to Oregon's fertile Willamette Valley spends considerable time and mileage in what is now Wyoming. This section of the trail was challenging and breathtaking, marked by notable landmarks that served as vital reference points for travelers and, today, stand as monuments to a bygone era of American expansion.

Independence Rock

Located in present-day Natrona County, Independence Rock is an enormous granite outcropping covering nearly 130 acres. Its name derives from the pioneers' benchmark to reach this point by July 4th, Independence Day, to ensure their caravan would avoid the treacherous mountain snows late in the journey. Over time, it became a tradition for travelers to inscribe their names on the rock, transforming it into a guestbook of sorts for those passing through.

Independence Rock by WonderPhotos.
https://pixabay.com/photos/independence-rock-storm-clouds-sky-7918622/

South Pass

Lying at an elevation of 7,550 feet, the South Pass is a wide and comparatively low saddle in the Rocky Mountains, facilitating the migration of thousands of settlers. Its significance cannot be overstated. Without South Pass's relatively gentle gradients, the westward migration via wagon might have taken a different trajectory altogether. It was key to the Oregon Trail's viability.

Devil's Gate

A striking, narrow cleft in the Rattlesnake Mountains, Devil's Gate stands about 370 feet tall and is a mere 1,500 feet long. The Sweetwater River flows through this gorge, but the pioneers, with their bulky wagons, had to bypass the actual gate. However, it served as an unmistakable landmark, guiding travelers and confirming they were on the correct path westward.

Register Cliff

Situated near Guernsey, Register Cliff is another "register of the desert," akin to Independence Rock. Settlers would carve their names, dates of passage, and sometimes brief messages into the soft sandstone. These inscriptions served as both a testament to their journey and a message to those who followed.

While vital navigation aids for 19th-century pioneers, these landmarks are more than just historical waypoints. They are tangible connections to the past, offering a window into the experiences, challenges, and aspirations of the thousands who journeyed westward. Today, as visitors traverse Wyoming's landscapes, these sites serve as poignant reminders of the state's integral role in shaping the American West. Each stone, cliff, and pass whispers of their tales of endurance, hope, and the relentless human drive to venture into the unknown.

Forts and Outposts on the Oregon Trail in Wyoming

Wyoming, with its unpredictable weather and challenging terrain, presented formidable obstacles to the pioneers journeying west and the fur traders before them. However, amidst these challenges, a series of forts and outposts emerged as crucial lifelines, offering respite, supplies, and sometimes even cultural exchange. These establishments, primarily built by traders, the US military, and settlers, provided structure and support on an otherwise precarious journey.

Fort Laramie

We cannot discuss Wyoming's forts without first returning to Fort Laramie. Originally established as Fort William in 1834 by fur traders, it underwent several transitions, culminating in its acquisition by the U.S. Army in 1849. The fort rapidly became a central point on the Oregon Trail. Whether pioneers needed supplies, a place to take a momentary respite, or simply the comfort of a little civilization amidst the wilderness, Fort Laramie stood as a beacon.

Fort Bridger

Established in 1843 by the renowned mountain man Jim Bridger, Fort Bridger lay in the southwest corner of Wyoming. Recognizing the need for services along the trail, Bridger initially set up the fort as a trading post. It provided blacksmithing services, essential supplies, and livestock trading options for passing pioneers. As the Mormons began settling in Utah, Fort Bridger became a significant point of interaction between them and other travelers.

Fort Casper

Originally known as Platte Bridge Station, Fort Casper was near present-day Casper, Wyoming. Established by the military in 1862, its primary purpose was to protect the telegraph line and the bridge over the North Platte River, both essential for communication and travel. The fort witnessed several skirmishes between Native American tribes and

US forces, reflecting the larger tensions as westward expansion encroached upon indigenous territories.

Fort Reno

Near Powder River, Fort Reno was founded in the late 1860s in response to conflicts between settlers and Native Americans, particularly during what came to be known as Red Cloud's War. While its tenure as a military post was relatively brief, closing in 1868, its impact on ensuring the trail's safety during tumultuous times was undeniable.

La Prele Creek Post

Lesser-known but still essential, La Prele Creek Post was established by traders in the 1850s. While it wasn't a military fort, this trading post played a vital role by offering goods and supplies to the settlers. It stood as a testament to the symbiotic relationship between pioneers and traders, both of whom benefitted from the westward movement, albeit in different ways.

These forts and outposts, strategically scattered across Wyoming's vast landscapes, played multi-faceted roles. They offered tangible services like supplies and protection and functioned as social hubs where news was exchanged and cultures often met. For many travelers, these forts were islands of civilization amidst a sea of the unknown, providing psychological comfort besides the more tangible offerings. These establishments also bore witness to the darker side of westward expansion: land disputes, military engagements, and cultural clashes. Yet, their existence and stories remain integral to understanding the broader tapestry of the Oregon Trail and Wyoming's pivotal role in the westward saga.

Mormon Pioneer Trail in Wyoming

The westward expansion parallels stories of land opportunities and gold rushes. For some, it was a quest for religious freedom. The Mormon Pioneer Trail is a testament to a person's unyielding faith and pursuit of a place where they could practice their beliefs without persecution. Wyoming played a pivotal role in their journey, presenting both challenges and moments of grace.

The Church of Jesus Christ of Latter-day Saints, commonly referred to as the Mormon Church, faced significant opposition and violent confrontations in the eastern and central states. Their leader, Joseph Smith, was killed by a mob in Illinois in 1844. Following his death, Brigham Young took the mantle of leadership. Recognizing the pressing need for a haven, he directed the church's migration westward. Their journey, now known as the Mormon Pioneer Trail, spanned five states, including a significant portion of Wyoming.

Wyoming's stretch of the trail is characterized by its diverse terrains: vast prairies transitioning into rugged mountains and deep valleys. The trail entered Wyoming from the east, near the present-day town of Torrington, and proceeded westward through Fort Laramie.

Rocky Ridge and Martin's Cove

One of the most harrowing episodes in the history of the Mormon migration occurred in Wyoming. Late in the 1856 migration season, two handcart companies, led by James G. Willie and Edward Martin, found themselves stranded in a brutal snowstorm near Rocky Ridge. Ill-prepared for such conditions, many died from cold and exhaustion. The survivors sought shelter in nearby Martin's Cove, which now stands as a place of reflection and remembrance for those who perished and those who, through sheer will, survived.

As word of the stranded handcart companies reached Salt Lake City, Brigham Young immediately mobilized a rescue mission. Teams of men, equipped with supplies and wagons, journeyed through the Wyoming terrain, battling worsening winter conditions. Their timely arrival and the provisions they carried undoubtedly saved many lives. By the time the survivors reached Utah, Willie's company is estimated to have suffered around a 14 percent death rate and Martin's 25 percent.

Church Ferry and the Sweetwater River

Further along the trail, pioneers encountered the Sweetwater River, a crucial water source for both the Mormon Trail and the Oregon Trail but also a significant obstacle. The Mormon Church established a ferry service in the early 1850s to aid in crossing, reducing the risk and strain of fording the river, especially during periods of high water.

After crossing the Sweetwater, the pioneers faced the challenging ascents of the Rocky Mountains. Though daunting, these peaks symbolized the end of their journey through Wyoming and their imminent arrival in the Salt Lake Valley.

This was a spiritual journey. Every hill and valley, every river crossed or ridge climbed represented challenges faced and overcome, often at great personal cost. In their beauty and harshness, Wyoming's landscapes became a crucible of faith, resilience, and community.

Today, portions of the trails are still visible, and markers, monuments, and visitor centers dot the path, ensuring that the sacrifices and triumphs of those early pioneers are not forgotten.

Impact on Indigenous Peoples

The westward expansion of the United States in the 19th century, epitomized by trails such as the Oregon Trail and the Mormon Pioneer Trail, represented a hopeful journey for many. However, this movement was not without profound consequences, especially for the indigenous peoples who had long inhabited the lands these trails crossed. Wyoming, as a central point in the westward migration, saw its native inhabitants bear the brunt of these changes.

As we've covered in previous chapters, Wyoming was home to various tribes, including the Shoshone, Arapaho, Cheyenne, and Lakota. For these tribes, the land was not just a resource; it was intertwined with their identity, spirituality, and livelihood. The increasing flow of settlers disrupted traditional hunting grounds, and competition for resources escalated tensions.

Resources

The bison, a keystone of the Great Plains indigenous cultures, began to decline dramatically in numbers. Overhunting by settlers, coupled with the encroachment on grazing lands, put additional stress on the populations. For tribes that relied on bison for sustenance, clothing, shelter, and tools, this decline was not just an environmental concern but a threat to their way of life.

Treaties and Broken Promises

Efforts were made to manage the escalating tensions between settlers and native tribes, primarily through treaties. The Treaty of Fort Laramie in 1851 was a significant attempt to define territories for tribes and guarantee safe passage for settlers. However, these treaties were frequently violated by both sides. As gold was discovered in Montana, the Bozeman Trail, cutting through established tribal territories in Wyoming, became a hotspot of conflict.

Forced Relocations

As clashes intensified, the US government began implementing policies of forced relocation. They moved indigenous groups to reservations, often far from their ancestral lands. This policy culminated in the tragic event known as the Sand Creek Massacre of 1864, where a peaceful camp of Cheyenne and Arapaho Indians was attacked, leading to significant casualties.

Cultural Disruption

Beyond the immediate physical impact, the westward movement disturbed the cultural and spiritual fabric of indigenous societies. Their traditional way of life was upended. Many were compelled to adopt unfamiliar lifestyles, leading to a loss of cultural practices and knowledge.

It's crucial to acknowledge the resilience of these indigenous communities. Despite the manifold challenges, they preserved their identity, traditions, and stories, passing them down to subsequent generations. Today, their descendants continue to contribute vibrantly to Wyoming's cultural tapestry, ensuring that the legacy of their ancestors remains an integral part of the state's narrative.

In reflecting on the westward expansion and the trails that symbolize this movement, it's imperative to view the journey from the perspective of not just those who moved westward but those who were already there. Their stories, filled with sorrow and endurance, provide a more comprehensive understanding of Wyoming's history in the 19th century.

Chapter 4 – Territorial Wyoming (1800s)

As the grinding of wagon wheels in the ruts of time and the hopeful conversation of pioneers faded along the well-trodden trails of Wyoming, a new chapter in the region's history unfolded. Wyoming was transitioning from a conduit of westward movement to an established territory of the United States. The implications of this transformation were far-reaching, touching every facet of life in this region.

The designation of "territorial" status might imply a mere bureaucratic change, but for Wyoming, it represented a pivotal shift. Settlers were no longer just passing through; they were laying roots. The process of organizing a territory introduced a structured governance system and ushered in a wave of economic opportunities.

Yet, as with any major transformation, the road to the establishment of the Wyoming Territory was not without its challenges. The back and forth of political ambitions, the search for resources to financially support the new government, and the intersection of various cultural groups set the stage for a complex and compelling period in Wyoming's history.

Formation of the Oregon Territory

The North American West has always been typified by its diverse landscapes and hopes for riches from natural resources, and this idea was not lost on the early visionaries of the US. Oregon Country, the area now broken up into modern-day Oregon, Washington, Idaho, and parts of Montana, Wyoming, and British Columbia, was the focus of these aspirations for glory. The formation of the Oregon Territory is a tale of diplomacy, ambition, and the nation's hunger for expansion, directly related to the development of Wyoming.

For many years before its territorial establishment, Oregon Country was an area of shared interest and sometimes contention. Both the United States and Great Britain had claims in the region, with Russia and Spain also expressing earlier interest. Fur traders and early explorers from the British Hudson's Bay Company and American enterprises traversed the rivers, traded with indigenous populations, and established forts and trading posts.

By the early 1800s, American settlers driven by the promise of fertile lands traveled that arduous Oregon Trail. These emigrants, many spurred by economic difficulties in the East or the allure of free land in the West, increasingly viewed Oregon Country as an American destiny. Their presence only bolstered the United States' claim to the region.

However, political maneuverings to determine the fate of this vast territory required more delicate diplomacy. The Anglo-American Convention of 1818 initially established a "joint occupation" agreement, allowing citizens of both the US and Britain to settle in Oregon Country. But as American settlers poured into the region, outnumbering their British counterparts, the call for a clear division grew louder.

The 1840s saw increasing pressures within the US for a resolution. The slogan "Fifty-four Forty or Fight!" emerged, referencing the latitude 54°40' (54 degrees, 40 minutes) north as the desired northern boundary of American Oregon and hinting at the nation's willingness to go to war over the territory. Yet, pragmatism prevailed. Recognizing the realities on the ground and the potential costs of conflict, the US and Britain negotiated the Oregon Treaty in 1846. This treaty established the 49th parallel, excluding Vancouver Island, as the boundary between British and US holdings, formally dividing Oregon Country.

Within two years, President James K. Polk signed the Oregon Territory Act (August 14, 1848), officially establishing the Oregon Territory. This new territory stretched far beyond what we know today as the state of Oregon.

Though only a small portion of Wyoming's northern section was included in the Oregon Territory, this period was significant. The trails that had facilitated westward migration became more defined, and the political strategies surrounding the territory's formation highlighted Wyoming's position within the broader context of westward expansion. Over the following decades, Wyoming would undergo further political delineations. Still, its initial inclusion in the Oregon Territory underscored its integral role in the narrative of the American West.

The formation of the Oregon Territory was only the beginning and no simple political act. It was the culmination of decades of dreams, ambitions, and the ever-evolving identity of a young nation. For those who lived in this region, both the indigenous and the newcomers, it marked the start of a new era, with challenges and opportunities ahead.

The Fort Laramie Treaty

This idea of westward expansion and greener pastures peaked by the mid-1800s as the relationships between the indigenous peoples and the new settlers encroaching on their lands took center stage. One of the most significant efforts to "tame" these relationships was the Fort Laramie Treaty.

We've mentioned Fort Laramie before—the fur trading post turned military depot at the crossroads of major travel routes, including the Oregon and Mormon Trails. Once the US military took over, it also became the center of interactions between the US government and the Native American nations.

The waves of settlers, gold-seekers, and traders flowed into the indigenous territories, disrupting traditional ways of life and straining resources. Conflict was inevitable, and the US government quickly recognized the need for heavy intervention for peace and to delineate new territories.

In the fall of 1851, both the US government and several Plains tribes, including the Lakota Sioux, Cheyenne, Arapaho, Crow, Shoshone, Assiniboine, Mandan, Hidatsa, and Arikara, sent representatives to Fort Laramie for talks. This was one of the most monumental meetings of the time, with attendance measuring in the thousands. The idea was to allow for the discussion of grievances and aspirations.

The treaty that emerged had several key provisions. It acknowledged specific territorial boundaries for each tribe, ensuring, in theory, that they would respect one another's territorial sovereignty. Given the overlapping and fluid nature of traditional territories, this was no easy task. Moreover, the US government promised to pay annuities to the tribes, compensating for disruptions caused by the increasing flow of settlers along the trails. On the other hand, the tribes were to allow safe passage for the settlers and stop fighting the construction of military forts and roads.

As with many treaties of this kind, the Treaty of Fort Laramie was marked by ambiguities and lofty promises. While it recognized indigenous sovereignty over vast swaths of the Plains, it also marked the beginning of a more structured infringement on these lands. The very trails and forts it sought to protect would pave the way for more settlers, railways, and eventually more encroachments.

By the 1860s, as more settlers made their way west and gold was discovered in Montana, the pressures on indigenous lands and the treaty's stipulations intensified. Conflicts erupted, leading to a renegotiation in the 1868 Treaty of Fort Laramie, which notably established the Great Sioux Reservation. While beyond the scope of our discussion, this treaty underscores the fluidity and tension that marked US-indigenous relations during this period.

For Wyoming, the 1851 Treaty of Fort Laramie held significance. Portions of the state were recognized as territories for various tribes; at the same time, the treaty sanctioned the trails that brought settlers, trade, and eventually more permanent establishments within Wyoming's bounds.

It's essential to understand the dual nature of this treaty. On the one hand, it was an incredibly ambitious attempt to bring order to the Plains, acknowledging indigenous rights and seeking to curtail conflict. On the other hand, it was a product of the times, deeply seated in the US government's ambitions for westward expansions and control.

Violations and unfulfilled promises tainted the treaty, like its fellows, yet it remains a cornerstone of the history of the American West. It encapsulated the hopes, tensions, and challenges of a region undergoing rapid transformation and solidified Wyoming's place within this larger narrative.

Gold Rushes and Booms

Deeply entwined in the story of the American West is the lure of gold, the shimmering promise of fortune that beckoned many to the rugged landscapes. Wyoming, too, became part of this active period in the 19th century. Both frenzy and consequence marked the state's role in the broader American gold rush phenomenon.

The 1860s brought whispers of gold from the mountainous terrains of Wyoming. While the state's gold stories may not have reached the fame of California's or Alaska's, the impact on the region was no less profound. It began in 1867 with the discovery of gold in the Sweetwater River area. Prospectors converged on the South Pass region, and the rush was on.

These early discoveries played an important role in the region's dynamics. Before the 1860s, much of Wyoming was a land to pass through because of the major trails that crossed the countryside. However, gold transformed it into a destination. Towns like Atlantic City, South Pass City, and Miner's Delight sprang up almost overnight. While the term "boomtown" might evoke images of bustling streets and endless prosperity, many of these towns experienced short-lived booms, with populations swelling and then dramatically shrinking as the easily accessible gold was extracted and new prospects drew them elsewhere.

Despite their fleeting nature, these booms dramatically altered Wyoming's landscape. Infrastructure in the form of roads and rudimentary railways carved its way into the wilderness. These initial trails and routes, borne of gold fever, would lay the groundwork for more significant transportation and communication networks in the following years.

It wasn't only the physical landscape that felt the weight of the gold rushes. The social fabric of Wyoming shifted, as well. A predominantly male population of miners brought the trappings of frontier life: saloons, gambling dens, and the inevitable tensions that arise in boomtown settings. It also marked the beginning of more structured communities, with schools, newspapers, and other civic establishments taking root.

Of course, there was an impact on the indigenous communities. As with many gold rushes across the US, the influx of miners and settlers led to disputes over land and resources. Many tribes, already grappling with the repercussions of treaties like Fort Laramie, found themselves further marginalized. The quest for gold intensified the pressures they faced, leading to displacements and conflicts.

But gold was just the beginning. In the latter part of the 19th century, Wyoming's mineral wealth diversified. While the gold booms may have dwindled, the discovery of other precious minerals, including copper, silver, and emerald, ensured that Wyoming's mineral story was far from over. These discoveries, coupled with the onset of coal mining, positioned Wyoming as a region rich in mineral resources. Towns like Hartville, with its copper mines, and Diamondville, known for coal, showcased Wyoming's burgeoning status as a mineral powerhouse.

Throughout history, gold rushes are often remembered for the individual stories of rags to riches, of prospectors transformed overnight into millionaires. While these tales are captivating, the real legacy of such events, particularly in Wyoming, lies in the broader changes they set in motion. Pursuing that shimmering metal in the state's rivers and mountains was more than just a quest for personal wealth; it was a chapter in the transformation of a region, setting Wyoming on a path of growth and evolution.

Territorial Government and Politics

When discussing the formative years of Wyoming's territorial period, we cannot sidestep the intricate play of politics and governance. By the 1860s, as settlers, miners, and entrepreneurs carved out niches in the region's rugged terrain, the necessity for a structured system of governance became abundantly clear. Wyoming's transition from an unorganized wilderness to a defined political entity was not without hurdles, but it played a pivotal role in shaping the state's identity.

The Organic Act, signed into law by President Ulysses S. Grant in 1868, officially established Wyoming Territory. This legislative act was the blueprint for Wyoming's territorial government, laying out the structure and mechanics of its political system. It delineated the roles of key officers, including a governor, secretary, and three-member judicial body, all of whom were presidential appointees.

The establishment of a territorial structure was only the beginning. Wyoming's political landscape in these early years was nothing short of dynamic. The territory's vast expanse, coupled with its sparse population, posed unique challenges. The scattered and often isolated communities needed representation, yet the sheer size of the territory made centralized governance a logistical challenge.

A significant milestone in Wyoming's political maturation came in 1869 with the convening of the first territorial legislature. This body, consisting of a Council and House of Representatives, was tasked with crafting the laws and policies that would guide Wyoming during its territorial phase.

While some issues they tackled were universal to many U.S. territories of the time, such as infrastructure development and land management, others were distinctive to Wyoming. One such issue was women's suffrage. In a move that was both groundbreaking and pragmatic, the 1869 legislature granted women the right to vote. The decision, influenced by a desire to bolster the territory's population and perhaps earn statehood, placed Wyoming at the forefront of the women's suffrage movement in the US.

But it wasn't just voting rights that showcased Wyoming's progressive leanings. The territory also saw the country's first female justice of the peace and a notable focus on education, with policies ensuring that both boys and girls had access to schooling.

Yet, territorial politics wasn't without its tensions. The very nature of a frontier, with its mix of indigenous populations, settlers, miners, and ranchers, meant that competing interests often came to a head. Land use, mineral rights, and interactions with Native American tribes were sources of continual debate. There were also internal disputes to contend with. Cheyenne, chosen as the territorial capital in 1869, faced competition from other locales vying for this prestigious title. The choice of Cheyenne, with its advantageous position on the Union Pacific Railroad, underscored the significance of transportation and commerce in the territory's political considerations.

Another element that shaped Wyoming's territorial politics was its relationship with the federal government. As a territory, Wyoming was essentially a ward of the federal government, reliant on it for key appointments and financial support. This dynamic created a push-and-pull scenario, with Wyomingites seeking greater autonomy and self-governance while navigating the confines of territorial status.

By the close of the 1880s, as discussions of statehood began to gain traction, Wyoming's political landscape had evolved considerably from its early territorial days. It had experienced the complexities of frontier governance, grappled with its identity, and set the stage for its eventual transition to statehood.

Wyoming's territorial political journey offers a fascinating glimpse into the challenges and opportunities of frontier governance. While the backdrop was distinctive to Wyoming—with its vast landscapes and unique demographic makeup—the themes are universally American: the pursuit of representation, the balance of local versus central governance, and the quest for a distinct identity within the broader tapestry of the nation.

Wyoming's Role in the Civil War

At a glance, Wyoming's involvement in the Civil War is a bit vague. After all, the territory itself was not officially established until 1868, three years after the war's conclusion. However, a closer examination reveals that the region that would become Wyoming was not untouched by the events of the 1860s.

The broader geopolitical significance of the western territories during the Civil War era cannot be understated. The struggle for control over these territories between the Union and the Confederacy was, in many ways, a struggle for the nation's future trajectory. Both sides recognized the vast potential of the West, be it in terms of resources, strategic value, or symbolic importance.

While no major battles were fought on Wyoming soil, the region experienced the war's ripple effects. The most immediate of these was the presence of military personnel. Union troops were stationed in the area to protect the crucial transportation routes, like the Overland Trail, from potential Confederate raids. These troops also protected settlers and stagecoach routes from potential threats, including indigenous tribes seeking to defend their lands from encroaching settlers.

Many individuals who settled in Wyoming during and after the war were veterans, drawn by the promise of land and opportunity. Their experiences in the war invariably influenced their approach to frontier life, infusing the budding communities with a blend of martial discipline and a desire for peaceful prosperity.

Economically, the Civil War also indirectly impacted Wyoming's development. With the nation's focus largely on the war, the push for westward expansion slowed. However, post-war, there was a renewed vigor to settle and develop the western territories, leading to an influx of people and capital into areas like Wyoming. The construction of the transcontinental railroad, a project accelerated in the post-war period, was pivotal in this respect.

In a more intangible sense, the Civil War's ideals and conflicts—the struggles over states' rights, federal power, and, most profoundly, slavery—echoed in Wyoming's early political and social conversations. While Wyoming was far removed from the epicenters of these debates, the territory grappled with related issues, especially governance, rights, and the role of the federal government.

While Wyoming's direct engagement with the Civil War was limited, its indirect interactions were profound. The war shaped the territory's economic, social, and political currents, playing a foundational role in Wyoming's journey from a frontier territory to an integral part of the Union.

Impact of the Transcontinental Railroad on Territorial Wyoming

When the Golden Spike was driven at Promontory Summit, Utah, in 1869, it symbolically knitted the United States together. The transcontinental railroad, this marvel of engineering and determination, had profound implications for the country, and nowhere was this felt more keenly than in the territory of Wyoming.

The most immediate and clear impact on Wyoming was economic. The railroad transformed the territory from a relatively remote frontier to a key junction, facilitating the movement of goods, people, and ideas. Cities like Cheyenne, which became a primary hub for the Union Pacific Railroad, witnessed exponential growth. From a transient camp in 1867, Cheyenne transformed into the most populous city in Wyoming by 1870, driven primarily by the railroad and its associated industries.

The rapid influx of settlers and capital brought its own challenges and opportunities. New communities emerged almost overnight, and with them came the need for infrastructure, governance, and law and order. While this hastened the process of statehood for Wyoming, it also led to conflicts over land, resources, and power. As settlers poured in, disputes with the region's indigenous inhabitants intensified, leading to tragic confrontations and further displacement of Native American tribes.

Another significant aspect of the railroad was the diversification it introduced to Wyoming's economy. Before the railroad, the territory relied primarily on raw materials like timber and minerals. With the establishment of the transcontinental railroad, there was a surge in demand for coal, which Wyoming had in abundance. The mining towns of Rock Springs and Hanna became crucial suppliers for the steam engines that powered the trains.

The railroad facilitated the cattle boom in Wyoming. Ranchers could now transport their livestock to markets in the East far more efficiently. This brought prosperity to many in the territory but altered the landscape as ranching operations expanded and fenced the iconic open ranges of the West.

The transcontinental railroad served as a conduit for bringing diverse groups into Wyoming. Workers from different parts of the world, especially the Chinese laborers who played a vital role in the railroad's construction, added to the ethnic mosaic of the territory. While this diversity enriched Wyoming's culture, it also led to tensions, as seen in events like the Rock Springs Massacre of 1885, where racial animosities erupted in violence.

The railroad had lasting environmental implications. The increased movement of people and goods, combined with the industrial activities associated with the railroad, left an indelible mark on Wyoming's pristine landscapes. Tensions between development and conservation, a theme that would resonate throughout Wyoming's history in the modern era, can trace some of its origins to this period.

The railroad was more than just a marvel of engineering; it was a force that reshaped the social, economic, and environmental fabric of territorial Wyoming. The legacy of this railroad era is still palpable in Wyoming today, a testament to the profound changes it ushered in during the latter half of the 19th century.

Chapter 5 – The Wyoming Cattle Boom and Johnson County War (Late 1800s)

The sounds of cattle hooves on the open range marked the close of the 19th century in Wyoming and the tensions of a state rapidly evolving. As the country recovered from the Civil War and moved into an era of expansion, Wyoming stood on the cusp of significant change. The cattle industry, buoyed by high beef prices and vast stretches of public grazing land, took root in the Wyoming territory. This era, often romanticized by tales of cowboys and open ranges, was, in reality, a complex tapestry of economic ambition, class struggles, and the inevitable clash between small settlers and established cattle barons.

The cattle boom brought prosperity and a promise of stable growth for Wyoming. New towns emerged, and with them, new opportunities for trade and business. But as cattle numbers swelled and the stakes grew higher, conflicts over land and water rights, cattle rustling, and market control began to surface. The state's legal and political systems, still finding their footing, were tested as they grappled with the challenges posed by this booming industry. At the heart of these tensions was the Johnson County War, a pivotal event that encapsulated the broader conflicts of this period.

In this chapter, we delve into the intricacies of the Wyoming cattle boom, the characters who shaped it, the challenges they faced, and the profound impact of the Johnson County War on the state's identity and future trajectory. Through a nuanced exploration of events, we'll uncover the layered history of a state navigating the challenges of progress, prosperity, and power during one of its most transformative periods.

Ranching and Cattle Industry

Wyoming's vast grasslands, relatively mild winters, and access to water sources presented a nearly ideal environment for the cattle industry. The earliest cattle entrepreneurs were trailblazers in physical exploration and economic innovation. Texas longhorns were among the first breeds to grace Wyoming's open ranges. These cattle were hardy and well-suited to the rough terrains and extended journeys, often driven northward from Texas along well-established trails. The drives were long and perilous but proved profitable as the demand for beef skyrocketed in the northern and eastern states.

The nature of cattle ranching in Wyoming changed in the late 1870s and early 1880s. The days of long cattle drives began to wane with the advent and expansion of the railroad. This development ensured cattle could be transported faster and more efficiently to markets in Chicago and other major hubs. As a result, larger cattle operations began to settle permanently in Wyoming, marking the beginning of the "open range" ranching system.

This system relied heavily on Wyoming's vast tracts of public land, where cattle grazed freely without the confines of traditional fencing. Ranchers established their claims based on access to water sources, an essential element in the arid West, and the surrounding land was utilized for grazing. Without formal boundaries, it became vital for ranchers to identify their cattle, leading to the intricate art of branding. Brands became symbols of pride and identity, each unique and registered with the state.

As the cattle industry grew, so did the capital backing it. Eastern and British investors, drawn by tales of the West and the promise of high returns, poured money into these ventures. These cash influxes led to the establishment of some of the largest cattle operations Wyoming had ever seen. The larger outfits, often called "cattle barons," controlled vast territories and resources, becoming influential economic and political forces in the territory. Their fortunes were often built on a mix of shrewd business acumen, favorable policies, and, at times, aggressive tactics against competitors.

But ranching was not without its challenges. The severe winter of 1886-87 stands as a testament to the vulnerabilities of the cattle industry. Ill-prepared for the harsh conditions, vast numbers of cattle perished. This event was a turning point, pushing ranchers to rethink strategies and consider more sustainable practices, such as shifting from open grazing to fenced, sectioned ranches and introducing sturdier cattle breeds.

The growth of the cattle industry inevitably led to increased competition for land and resources. Small ranchers, or "grangers," often found themselves in contention with larger outfits. The big operators were perceived as having undue influence, often securing the best grazing spots and water sources, leaving smaller players struggling for the leftovers. This disparity sowed seeds of discontent and rivalry, setting the stage for conflicts that would mark Wyoming's cattle ranching history.

The cattle industry also significantly influenced Wyoming's social fabric. Towns like Cheyenne and Laramie became central trading and supply hubs, drawing merchants, workers, and even entertainers. Saloons, hotels, and shops sprung up, catering to the ranchers, cowboys, and visitors, bringing vibrancy and dynamism to these communities.

Wyoming's ranching and cattle industry was not just about herding and selling cattle. It encompassed the hopes and ambitions of a diverse group of people—from wealthy investors to hard-working cowboys, from large-scale barons to small ranchers. Their collective efforts and challenges, their triumphs and defeats, intricately twisted a rich part of Wyoming's ranching history, leaving an indelible mark on the state's economic, social, and political landscapes.

Cattle Barons and Outlaws

Wyoming in the late 19th century was a land of contrast where the ambitions of wealthy cattlemen intersected with the sometimes lawless frontiers of the West. The emergence of cattle barons and tales of notorious outlaws painted a vivid picture of a region undergoing rapid transformation.

Cattle Barons

The cattle barons played a pivotal role in Wyoming's economy. They were not merely ranchers but key players in regional trade networks, connecting Wyoming's beef to markets in the East and even overseas. Towns and infrastructure often grew around their operations, and they employed a significant portion of the state's labor force in various capacities.

With great wealth came social influence. The barons built grand homes, patronized the arts, and sometimes even dabbled in politics. Organizations like the Wyoming Stock Growers Association (WSGA), dominated by these magnates, played influential roles in territorial governance and establishing industry norms.

Yet, their ascendancy was not without its dark chapters. The Johnson County War, as discussed briefly, highlighted the lengths to which some cattle barons would go to maintain their economic dominance. Moreover, their vast landholdings often came at the expense of smaller ranchers, Native American tribes, and the environment.

Outlaws

Wyoming's vast and rugged terrain, combined with its position at the crossroads of major trails and railways, made it an appealing backdrop for outlaws. These individuals, often disillusioned by society or seeking quick fortunes, operated on the fringes of the law. While some were genuine criminals, they painted others as outlaws because of disputes, misunderstandings, or political maneuvering.

Wyoming's outlaw history boasts a roster of colorful characters. While they were undoubtedly criminals, tales of their exploits, camaraderie, and occasional acts of generosity added a romantic tint to their narrative.

The life of an outlaw in Wyoming was not one of luxury. They often navigated treacherous landscapes, faced threats from lawmen and rival criminals, and lived in hiding. Places like the Hole-in-the-Wall, a remote valley in Wyoming, became infamous as outlaw hideouts, offering natural protection against pursuers.

Hole-in-the-Wall, Wyoming by 12019.
https://pixabay.com/photos/hole-in-the-wall-wyoming-valley-72350/

The turn of the century brought increased law enforcement capabilities and infrastructure development to Wyoming. These changes, coupled with a societal shift that no longer romanticized outlaw behavior, marked the decline of the traditional outlaw era. However, their legacy persisted in tales, songs, and films that romanticized the "Wild West."

The dynamics between cattle barons and outlaws in late 19th century Wyoming present a study in contrasts. The barons, with their vast resources and often formalized structures, represented the establishment and the march of progress. Outlaws symbolized resistance to this march, harking back to an older, wilder vision of the West.

Yet, both groups were integral to Wyoming's history. They highlighted the dichotomies of a state caught between tradition and progress, lawfulness and rebellion, and economic growth and preservation. Through their stories, we gain insights into the complex socio-economic and cultural forces at play in a pivotal era of Wyoming's development.

Butch Cassidy in Wyoming

Wyoming's past has seen more than its fair share of tales, but few are as enduring as that of Butch Cassidy, born Robert LeRoy Parker. In the latter part of the 19th century, as Wyomingites went about their daily lives, whispers often traveled about the deeds of the "Wild Bunch" gang, led by none other than Cassidy himself.

The Hole-in-the-Wall pass in Johnson County became a near-mythical hideout, with stories painting it as an impregnable fortress for outlaws. From this secluded spot, Cassidy and his gang meticulously planned their heists. They struck banks and trains with precision, often leaving lawmen scratching their heads and towns buzzing with the audacity of the raids.

However, in local taverns and around campfires, another narrative emerged that contrasted sharply with his criminal exploits. Here, Cassidy wasn't just an outlaw; he was a symbol of resistance against the encroaching powers of the East, a man who stood up to the corporate railroads and wealthy bankers. He was known to slip coins into the hands of a struggling rancher or ensure a widow had enough to get by. To many in Wyoming, especially the poor and marginalized, Cassidy was their Robin Hood.

When tales of his generosity reached law enforcement, they were often met with skepticism. Yet, in towns where the Wild Bunch had passed through, children would speak of candy bought with coins Cassidy had given them. Families remembered when they were on the brink, only to find an envelope with the exact amount needed to save their homes.

To truly understand Butch Cassidy's place in Wyoming's history, we must look beyond the wanted posters and newspaper headlines. Instead, we focus on the local stories, the gratitude of those he helped, and the rugged landscapes of Wyoming that sheltered him. In these tales, Cassidy emerges not as just an outlaw but a complex figure who, in his own way, tried to right the wrongs he saw in the world.

The Sundance Kid (Harry Alonzo Longabaugh)

Among the tales of outlaws and lawmen, one name stands out with a particular resonance: the Sundance Kid, or as some knew him, Harry Alonzo Longabaugh. While his exploits alongside Butch Cassidy have become the stuff of legend, it was the personal ties and rugged landscape of Wyoming that gave him an identity.

With its backdrop of mountains and plains, the town of Sundance might seem like any other small settlement in Wyoming. But for Longabaugh, it held a pivotal chapter in his life. There, in the shadows of the Bear Lodge Mountains, a young Harry found himself behind bars, paying for a youthful indiscretion of horse theft. The time he spent there, the isolation and the introspection, led him to adopt the town's name as his own. Perhaps it was a nod to a turning point in his life or an ironic twist of fate. Whatever the reason, "Sundance Kid" was born.

People saw more than just an outlaw when they looked at the Sundance Kid. Sure, he had his fair share of wrongdoings, but those close to him in the Wyoming taverns and back alley meetings described a different side. It wasn't just about his sharpshooting—it was the twinkle in his eye, the way he could light up a room. When he teamed up with Butch Cassidy, their adventures became the stuff of local legends. But behind the headlines of their daring escapades were stories of deep friendships, unwavering loyalty, and surprising acts of kindness.

Wyoming, with its expansive plains, hidden valleys, and tight-knit communities, served as both a backdrop and a participant in Sundance's life. It offered him refuge, challenges, and a canvas on which his legend was painted. While the wider world may remember him for the heists and the headlines, in Wyoming, the Sundance Kid is remembered in a more nuanced light: a man shaped by his environment who, in turn, left an indelible mark on the state's rich tapestry of history.

Tom Horn

Few figures loom as large or as enigmatic as Tom Horn. A man whose life straddled the line between law and lawlessness, Horn's story is one of grit, ambiguity, and the complex morality of the Wild West.

Starting as an army scout, Tom learned the nuances of the terrain, becoming adept at tracking and understanding the often unpredictable nature of the land and its inhabitants. However, as times changed, so did Horn's role. The cattle wars, a tumultuous period marked by land disputes, rustling, and violent skirmishes, drew him into a darker side of the frontier.

Working for the powerful Wyoming Stock Growers Association, Horn took on the role of a detective. But he wasn't just any detective; he was an enforcer, a tangible presence of the association's might. With a steely gaze and an uncompromising approach, he pursued those who threatened the interests of the cattle barons. To some, he was a necessary protector, upholding the rights of the ranchers. To others, he was a menace, his methods often skirting the boundaries of the law.

The line between hero and villain blurred further with the tragic death of Willie Nickell, a young boy caught in the crossfire of the ever-intensifying cattle wars. Rumors swirled, whispers abounded, and fingers pointed in Horn's direction. The trial that unfolded was as much about Horn's involvement in the boy's death as it was the reflection of a region grappling with its own identity. Was Wyoming to be a place where might made right, or was it time for the rule of law to assert itself?

Tom Horn's execution, whether seen as justice served or a scapegoat's fate, undeniably marked a profound shift. The cattle wars, with their raw display of power struggles and territorial disputes, began to wane, making room for a new era. But in saloons, around family hearths, and under the expansive Wyoming sky, the legacy of Tom Horn, a man who embodied the wild complexities of the West, continues to be fervently debated.

Cattle Kate (Ella Watson)

Here emerged a figure who defied the conventional molds of her time: Ella Watson, more commonly known as "Cattle Kate." A determined woman with an indomitable spirit, she found herself caught up in the intricate web of land rights, a fierce battleground where the mighty cattle barons held sway.

Ella didn't start with a desire for notoriety. Her aim was modest: to carve out a space for herself and her partner, James Averell, in this ever-expanding frontier. But in a landscape where land was both wealth and power, their aspirations brought them into direct conflict with those who held the reins of influence.

The charges leveled against her—cattle rustling—were more a reflection of the times than her actions. It was an era where rumors flew faster than truth, where one's fate could be sealed by whispers and innuendos. With no trial and no chance to clear their names, Ella and James met the grim fate of lynching at the hands of vigilantes.

Johnson County War: Causes and Outcomes

The Johnson County War, sometimes termed the "Cattle War," was more than a little regional skirmish in Wyoming's history. It symbolized the larger socio-economic and political struggles at play in the American West during the late 19th century. At its heart, this conflict was rooted in tensions between large cattle barons and smaller ranchers against the backdrop of an evolving economic landscape in Wyoming.

Causes

As previously discussed, the growth of the cattle industry in Wyoming led to heightened competition for grazing lands. Large-scale cattlemen aimed to monopolize prime grazing areas, especially those surrounding water sources. In contrast, smaller ranchers and homesteaders sought their share of the expansive Wyoming range. The open-range system, with its lack of fencing, only exacerbated these land disputes.

Theft of livestock, or rustling, became a significant concern for both large and small cattle operations. Larger outfits often accused smaller ranchers of rustling, sometimes without substantial evidence. The branding system, while useful, wasn't foolproof, and disputes over cattle ownership were frequent.

Because of their considerable economic weight, the larger cattle barons naturally wielded significant influence on the territorial government and legal systems. Through the WSGA, they often secured favorable laws and regulations, much to the chagrin of smaller operators.

Finally, the late 1880s were challenging times for cattle ranchers. Market prices for beef were fluctuating, and events like the harsh winter of 1886-87 dealt a significant blow to many large and small cattle outfits. These economic pressures heightened the stakes in the ongoing disputes.

The Outbreak of Conflict

The tension culminated in April 1892 when a group of cattlemen, hired guns, and detectives, backed by the WSGA, created a "hit list" of supposed rustlers and sympathizers in Johnson County. Known as "The Invaders," they set out to eliminate this perceived threat, leading to skirmishes, sieges, and the loss of several lives.

One of the most notable confrontations was the siege of the TA Ranch. The invaders hunkered down, surrounded by a posse of locals determined to defend their land and rights. This standoff lasted for days, with neither side willing to yield.

The conflict drew national attention. Finally, President Benjamin Harrison, realizing the gravity of the situation and fearing a larger civil conflict, dispatched federal troops to quell the skirmish. Their intervention led to the arrest of The Invaders, marking the official end of hostilities.

Outcomes

The captured invaders were taken to Cheyenne for trial. However, because of their influence and the complexities of the legal system, none of them were convicted. This outcome left many in Johnson County disillusioned with the territorial and federal justice system.

While the cattlemen may have won in the court, public opinion was less kind. The events of the Johnson County War diminished the influence and standing of the WSGA and the larger cattle barons in the region. The war had exposed the extent to which they were willing to go to maintain their dominance, leaving a bitter taste in the mouths of many Wyoming residents.

The Johnson County War was a clear sign that the days of the open range system were numbered. It became evident that clearer regulations, boundaries, and a more systematic approach to cattle ranching were necessary. Over the years, fencing became more common, marking an end to the vast open ranges that had defined Wyoming for so long.

The war became deeply ingrained in Wyoming's collective memory and culture. It highlighted the age-old American conflict between the "little guy" and large, powerful entities. Stories, songs, and films were inspired by these events, ensuring that the lessons and legends of the Johnson County War lived on.

The Johnson County War manifested the stresses and strains of a rapidly evolving Wyoming. It was a reminder of the challenges of westward expansion and the inevitable clashes that arose in the quest for resources, power, and economic stability. The lessons from this conflict are a testament to the resilience and determination of the people of Wyoming, shaping the state's identity and values for years to come.

Legacy of the Cattle Boom

Wyoming's cattle boom, while a defining era, was not merely a period confined to the annals of history. The events, characters, and changes it brought have had a lasting impact, shaping Wyoming's culture, economy, and environment in ways that resonate even today.

Economic Implications

The initial attraction to cattle ranching laid the groundwork for a diversified agricultural sector. While the dominance of cattle ranching waned, it paved the way for sheep herding, hay production, and other agricultural endeavors. The infrastructure, knowledge, and skills developed during the boom contributed to these offshoots.

The cattle boom influenced Wyoming's land ownership structures. Large ranches established by cattle barons continued, sometimes subdivided or reorganized. These patterns have implications for present-day land use, agricultural practices, and even conservation efforts.

Socio-Cultural Legacy

The skills and talents required of cowhands during the cattle boom found a new stage in the form of rodeos. Wyoming's rodeo culture, now recognized worldwide, is rooted in the cattle era. Events like Cheyenne Frontier Days, established in the late 19th century, can trace their origins to the heyday of the cattle industry.

The image of the cowboy, central to American identity, owes much to this period. Wyoming's cattle era crystallized the notion of the cowboy as a rugged, independent, and honorable figure. This archetype, propagated in literature, film, and art, holds a romanticized but critical place in American cultural consciousness.

Towns that sprang up as hubs for cattle trade or as points along the cattle driving routes often persisted. Their histories, local traditions, and even annual celebrations often hark back to the cattle boom era.

Environmental Considerations

Intensive cattle ranching, especially during the boom, had definitive environmental effects. Overgrazing in certain areas led to soil erosion and altered local ecosystems. In response, land management practices, regulations, and ranching techniques have sought to address and mitigate these impacts.

The cattle boom also influenced wildlife patterns. As ranchers sought to protect their herds, they sometimes came into conflict with native species like wolves and bears. This set the stage for early wildlife conservation dialogues in the state.

Political and Legal Foundations

In a region where water could be scarce, the cattle industry played a pivotal role in shaping Wyoming's water rights policies. Prioritizing access for agriculture, especially cattle ranching, these laws and regulations have had long-term implications for resource allocation in the state.

The extensive nature of cattle ranching operations brought about the need for clear land use policies and regulations. These early policies set precedents for future land use debates and decisions in Wyoming. With its distinct hierarchies and sometimes contentious relations between ranch owners, cowhands, and competing agricultural interests (like sheep herders), the cattle industry contributed to Wyoming's labor laws and dynamics.

The legacy of Wyoming's cattle boom is intricate, touching nearly every facet of the state's identity. Perhaps its most compelling legacy lies in its testament to Wyoming's adaptability. While honoring its history, the state has consistently demonstrated the ability to evolve, learn from the past, and chart a course that respects its heritage and future aspirations. With its profound impacts and subsequent adjustments, the cattle boom was a poignant chapter in this ongoing narrative.

Chapter 6 – Women's Suffrage in Wyoming (Late 1800s)

One aspect of Wyoming's history perhaps shines brighter than even the gold rush: the pioneering adoption of women's suffrage. Long before it became a cause for the women of the nation, Wyoming granted women the right to vote and play an active role in civic life.

The economic, cultural, and political landscape of the time profoundly influenced this early stance taken by the territory. While the West is often perceived as rugged and masculine, its realities demanded some of the more traditional gender roles be dissolved. The amount of wilderness in the territory, the sparser population, and the shared challenges of frontier life underscored a greater need for unity, collaboration, and mutual respect among its inhabitants.

In Chapter 6, we'll explore the important milestones and pivotal figures that shaped this early movement, as well as the broader implications of the movement for the future state of Wyoming and the rest of the country. How did Wyoming, a frontier state with its own set of challenges, come to the forefront of such transformative change? And how did this decision reverberate beyond the territory's borders and contribute to the larger push for women's rights across the country?

Wyoming's Role as the "Equality State"

The title "Equality State" that Wyoming proudly bears today isn't a mere coincidence; it's an emblem of the state's progressive stance toward gender rights, especially during a time when such perspectives were unconventional. Wyoming's adoption of this moniker traces back to its pioneering decision to grant women the right to vote in 1869, over half a century before the 19th Amendment extended this right nationwide.

Understanding why Wyoming was the first territory (and state) to take this step requires a multifaceted exploration into its demographics, economic imperatives, and political landscape. For one, the territorial period saw a stark gender imbalance. Men vastly outnumbered women, making it challenging to establish and sustain communities in what they perceived as a rugged frontier. Encouraging women to migrate to the region and actively participate in community-building was an implicit goal. Some saw granting women the right to vote as a potential incentive, emphasizing the territory's commitment to recognizing women as full citizens.

The spirit of the West was a unique one. In its vast landscapes, where nature's challenges demanded grit and cooperation, the roles men and women played rarely fit neatly into the boxes society had crafted. Out there, amidst the backdrop of rugged terrain and expansive skies, women were far more than just the caretakers of hearth and home. They wore multiple hats—they ran businesses, imparted knowledge as teachers, healed as nurses, and proudly claimed and stewarded land. Their hands, weathered by work and care, helped to weave the very fabric of their communities. In the West, every individual, regardless of gender, played their part in painting a larger, collaborative picture. Arguments for women's suffrage in Wyoming were as much about equity as they were about acknowledging the simple realities of life in the territory.

It's essential to note that not all support was ideologically driven. A distinct pragmatism marked the political atmosphere of Wyoming. Some legislators believed that endorsing women's suffrage would attract national attention and potentially expedite the journey to statehood. Some whispered that it was all just a political game, suggesting that Wyoming's newly enfranchised women might conveniently tilt their votes toward the favors of certain parties out of sheer gratitude.

Yet, behind every whisper, speculation, and eyebrow raised in surprise, the undeniable fact stood: On December 10, 1869, Wyoming cast a bold and pioneering light on the map as the trailblazer for women's suffrage in the US. As news spread, reactions varied wildly across the nation. Some papers praised the audacity, while others scratched their heads or downright scoffed. But whatever the take,

Wyoming had firmly staked its claim on history's pages. Wyoming remained steadfast. When the U.S. Congress suggested Wyoming might be denied statehood unless it revoked women's suffrage, the territory, displaying remarkable grit, replied that it would rather remain out of the Union than do so.

Wyoming's early commitment to gender equality wasn't without its challenges or critics. But through a blend of pragmatism, political maneuvering, and genuine progressive ideology, the territory established a legacy that would influence the trajectory of women's rights in America and enshrine its reputation as the "Equality State." This commitment was reaffirmed in 1890 when Wyoming entered the Union and ensured that its state constitution continued to grant women the right to vote, emphasizing its unyielding commitment to the principles of equality.

Women's Suffrage Movement

The story of women's suffrage in Wyoming may have been advanced but was still in sync with the broader national movement for gender equality. Spearheaded by resolute women and their allies, this ambitious path marked a transformative period in US history, characterized by peaceful and aggressive debates, strategic activism, and profound social change.

The national women's suffrage movement can trace its roots to the mid-19th century. The Seneca Falls Convention of 1848, organized by Elizabeth Cady Stanton and Lucretia Mott, is often hailed as its starting point. The convention's "Declaration of Sentiments," a groundbreaking document, laid out a comprehensive vision of women's rights, central to which was the demand for the right to vote.

As the 19th century progressed, various suffrage associations and societies sprang up across the nation. Women like Susan B. Anthony, Lucy Stone, and Sojourner Truth became iconic figures, tirelessly advocating for women's rights on and off the public stage. Their approaches varied: some focused on achieving suffrage at a state level, while others pursued a federal amendment. These strategic differences sometimes led to fractures within the movement but also catalyzed diverse and broad-reaching efforts.

Though geographically distant from these epicenters of activism, Wyoming was not insulated from their influence. Newspapers and periodicals brought news of national events and arguments for and against women's suffrage into Wyoming homes. Furthermore, the migration of people across the territories meant that ideas traveled, bringing debates and discussions surrounding women's rights.

It would be a grave mistake to assume that every woman in Wyoming or the nation was in favor of women's suffrage. The movement faced considerable opposition, not only from men who believed it would disrupt the societal order but also from women. These women felt that their influence in the private sphere was substantial and that formal political involvement might undermine this power.

The national movement faced numerous setbacks. Attempts to introduce a federal women's suffrage amendment were repeatedly thwarted. But the suffragists were undeterred. They adopted varied tactics, from publishing pamphlets and newspapers to organizing parades and protests. They also took legal routes. Susan B. Anthony famously voted illegally in 1872 and faced a subsequent trial, using the courtroom as a platform to promote the cause.

Against this backdrop, Wyoming's decision to grant women the vote in 1869 stood out as a beacon. Wyoming's early adoption of women's suffrage was celebrated by suffragists nationwide as a significant win. It provided tangible proof that women's enfranchisement was achievable and beneficial. Notably, when Esther Morris became the nation's first female Justice of the Peace in 1870 in South Pass City, Wyoming, it offered a compelling counter-narrative to those who doubted women's capability of holding office.

The dialogue between local actions in Wyoming and the broader national movement was undeniable. Wyoming's successes offered hope to suffragists elsewhere, while the challenges and strategies of the national movement gave Wyoming's women a broader context and support network.

The efforts of all eventually paid off in the passage of the 19th Amendment in 1920, granting women across the United States the right to vote. It becomes evident that the story of women's suffrage was woven with threads of local endeavors and national efforts. Each strand, whether from the bustling streets of New York or the rugged terrains of Wyoming, contributed to a larger narrative of resilience, determination, and the unyielding pursuit of equality.

The Wyoming Territorial Legislature

Formed in 1869, after Wyoming was designated a US territory, the 1st Wyoming Territorial Legislature faced the immense task of crafting laws for a region characterized by its diverse population and unique challenges. With its vast landscapes and sparse population, Wyoming required a legislative approach that acknowledged its distinctive nature.

Central to this legislature's early activities was the debate on women's suffrage. Women's suffrage was a contentious issue everywhere. While the broader American suffrage movement was gaining momentum, few could have predicted that Wyoming would be the first territory or state to grant women the right to vote.

In December 1869, William Bright, a saloonkeeper and legislator from South Pass City, introduced a bill to grant women suffrage. Bright, influenced by the suffragists in his life, notably his wife Julia, recognized women's essential role in frontier communities. He and others who supported the bill believed that enfranchising women was not only a matter of principle but also a pragmatic approach to attract more settlers to the territory.

Debate on the bill was vigorous. Some legislators voiced concerns that aligning with such a radical cause would invite ridicule. Others expressed doubt about women's suitability for political participation. But the bill's supporters, with logical arguments and driven by their sense of fairness, won. When the bill was presented to Governor John A. Campbell, he promptly signed it into law.

The decision wasn't without its detractors. Critics outside Wyoming attacked the move, sometimes dismissively attributing it to the territory's "thin air." Yet, the Wyoming Territorial Legislature remained steadfast. The positive impacts of women's enfranchisement soon became clear. When women began taking part in jury duties and offices, they showed their capability and enriched Wyoming's civic life with their perspectives.

The legislature's commitment to women's rights was further tested in 1871 when a bill was introduced to repeal women's suffrage. In a nail-biting vote, it defeated the bill, reinforcing its commitment to the principles of gender equality.

The Wyoming Territorial Legislature's actions during its early years reflect a blend of pragmatism, foresight, and a willingness to challenge prevailing norms, some would say ahead of their time. Granting women the right to vote uplifted half of the territory's population and solidified Wyoming's reputation as a trailblazer, forever shaping its identity as the "Equality State."

Key Figures in Wyoming's Suffrage Movement

While the story of women's suffrage in Wyoming was a collective endeavor, certain individuals stood out for their extraordinary commitment and influence.

Esther Hobart Morris

Esther Hobart Morris stands out as a beacon for women's rights and a testament to the grit and determination that typified the state's early settlers. Born into a time when women's roles were rigidly defined, Esther refused to be pigeonholed, breaking both barriers and conventions.

With its rugged charm and bustling mining operations, South Pass City witnessed the unfolding of Morris's pivotal role in the suffrage movement. Conversations over property rights, muddy trails, and the town's wooden storefronts started turning toward a radical idea: giving women the right to vote. And at the forefront of these debates was Esther, not just advocating but embodying the change she wished to see.

By 1870, her dedication culminated in a groundbreaking achievement: she donned the hat of the country's first female justice of the peace. Though her courtroom was a far cry from the grand halls of today, the judgments passed there carried the weight of change and symbolized the burgeoning hope for gender equality.

But beyond her notable titles and accolades, Esther Hobart Morris was a woman of substance and heart. Her life was a tapestry of challenges faced head-on and battles fought not just for herself but for every woman who came after her. Today, as Wyomingites reflect on their state's rich legacy of pioneering spirits, Esther's name resonates, reminding them of the strength, courage, and unwavering commitment to justice that remains the state's true hallmark.

Amalia Post

With her fiery spirit and articulate voice, Amalia Post was not just a participant in the suffrage movement; she was its very heartbeat. Born into a time of constrained expectations for women, Amalia refused to accept the status quo. Instead, she used her powerful and passionate voice to challenge prevailing norms and rally those around her to the cause of equality.

When Wyoming, with its expansive skies and untamed spirit, passed the suffrage act, it wasn't merely a local victory for Amalia. She saw it as a starting point, a spark that could ignite the fires of change across the nation. And so, with a heart full of conviction and a mission in her sights, she took to the roads, railways, and podiums beyond Wyoming's borders.

From the bustling streets of East Coast cities to the emerging towns in the Midwest, Amalia's voice resonated. She had an innate ability to connect with her audiences, weaving personal stories with the larger narrative of women's rights. Her words were not just speeches; they were calls to action, inspiring both men and women to imagine a nation where equality wasn't an ideal but a reality.

But for all her public presence, Amalia was also a woman of warmth and compassion. Those who had the privilege of knowing her spoke of her kindness, her genuine interest in their lives, and her unwavering belief in the potential of every individual. As her legacy continues to inspire, Amalia Post is a testament to the power of one voice, one vision, to effect monumental change.

Therese A. Jenkins

Therese A. Jenkins was more than just her titles; she was a movement in herself. While the rugged terrain of Wyoming was being shaped by winds and waters, Jenkins was shaping minds and opinions with equal vigor. At her core, she was an educator who believed in the transformative power of knowledge and the importance of equipping every individual with it.

As a teacher, she touched the lives of countless young minds, instilling in them academic lessons and life values. She taught them to question, challenge, and never settle for less than they deserved.

Stepping into the realm of newspaper editing, Jenkins found a larger classroom. Every column inch became an opportunity to enlighten, advocate, and inspire. She introduced her readers to the broader world of women's rights through her writings, weaving together global events with local implications. It was here she passionately argued for the importance of women's suffrage, painting a picture of a society enriched by the diverse voices of its members.

However, beyond her public roles, Jenkins was a person of profound depth and empathy. Those who knew her spoke of her listening skills, of evenings spent in deep conversations in which she would provide guidance, support, or a sympathetic ear. For many, she was not just an educator or editor but a mentor, a guiding light.

Therese A. Jenkins shines brightly. Through her dedication to education and relentless advocacy for women's rights, she carved out a legacy that still resonates today, reminding us of the change one determined individual can bring about.

Eliza Stewart Boyd

Eliza Stewart Boyd isn't just a name on a list; she was a catalyst in a period of profound transformation. In a time when women's voices were often hushed and their presence in civic spaces was merely ornamental, Eliza emerged as a beacon of change. As Wyoming's landscapes were marked by vast plains and towering peaks, its societal landscape was marked by figures like Boyd.

In 1870, when Eliza took her seat as a juror, it wasn't just a chair she occupied; it was a statement. Every glance she exchanged, every note she took, and every verdict she contributed to was a testament to the strides women were making in the public sphere. Her role on the jury wasn't simply about passing judgment on a specific case but about laying down a marker for future generations.

To her community, Eliza wasn't just another face in the jury box. She was the whisper of change on the horizon, a living proof that the winds of progress were stirring. Her friends, neighbors, and even the skeptics who raised eyebrows at women's voting rights could now see its tangible impact. Here was a woman, their very own Eliza, stepping into roles previously unimaginable.

And while many admired her from afar, there was an internal battle only Eliza knew. Every moment, she felt the profound weight of her place, the silent hopes of other women resting on her shoulders. It wasn't just about her; it was about the dreams and aspirations of so many others. Through her quiet strength, she showed them all a glimpse of a world where limitations fell away, replaced by newfound possibilities.

Today, when we think of Wyoming's legal and civic evolution, Eliza Stewart Boyd features prominently, not just for the history she made but for the path she illuminated for others to follow. Through her thoughtful presence in the quiet deliberation rooms of 1870, she echoed a message that resonated far and wide: women are not just spectators but vital contributors to the course of justice and progress.

Grace Raymond Hebard

Grace Raymond Hebard's story is one of grit wrapped in grace, a tale not just of historical significance but of heartfelt passion for the

American West and the rights of women. Born on the banks of the Mississippi in Clinton, Iowa, on a summer day in 1861, Grace grew up in a time of transformation and took that spirit of change into her very being.

Imagine a woman at the turn of the century, with a spark in her eye and an unstoppable drive, delving into dusty archives and trekking across the Wyoming plains to map the Oregon Trail. That was Grace. A professor who not only taught the dry facts of political economy but brought the stories of the West to life for her students. As the University of Wyoming's librarian, she didn't just catalogue books; she preserved the heartbeat of a state's history.

Her writings weren't mere academic exercises; they were acts of reclamation, bringing to light the overlooked roles of pioneering women who shaped the West. Her pen gave life to the stories of trailblazers, ensuring their names wouldn't be lost in the winds of time. And she didn't stop at writing history—she made it, by standing shoulder to shoulder with fellow suffragists, lecturing, advocating, and marching for the vote.

Picture her, a beacon of hope and determination, championing the story of Esther Hobart Morris as more than folklore, but as a testament to what women could achieve. It was Grace's relentless advocacy that secured Esther's place as a symbol of women's suffrage, a permanent reminder of the power of women in the public sphere.

And when she passed in the autumn of 1936, Grace Raymond Hebard left us more than a legacy; she left a blueprint of how to live fiercely, with conviction, in the pursuit of a fairer, more equitable world. Her life is a canvas, rich with the colors of academia, activism, and the unyielding wilds of Wyoming. She didn't just live in history; she wove herself into its very fibers, becoming as enduring as the rugged landscapes she so loved.

In your hands, her story unfolds, a vivid narrative that will guide readers through the complex dance of progress and tradition that is Wyoming's storied past.

Mary Bellamy

Mary Bellamy's foray into Wyoming politics wasn't just a personal triumph; it was a collective victory for women across the state and a beacon for the nation. As the first woman to warm a seat in the Wyoming State Legislature after her election in 1910, Bellamy shattered the glass ceiling with the same poise and determination with which she campaigned for office.

Bellamy's journey to the legislature was paved with the silent strength of countless women who, for decades, had advocated for the right to vote—a right that Wyoming had granted early on, serving as a trailblazer in women's suffrage. Yet, with the right to vote came the responsibility to lead, and lead she did. Her election was a testament to the confidence placed in women by Wyoming's progressive electorate and proof of the political maturity the state had reached.

Once in office, Bellamy was far from a silent member. She leveraged her platform to amplify the voices of those who had historically been silenced. With a firm belief in the upliftment of all citizens, she continued to advocate for the rights of women, understanding that the right to vote was just one battle in a larger war against inequality. Her legislative work reflected a commitment to education, healthcare, and child welfare—issues that touched the very fabric of everyday life for Wyoming's families.

Bellamy's tenure in politics transcended mere policy-making; it was about setting a precedent that a woman's place was wherever she chose it to be, including in the chambers of power. Her presence in the legislature sent ripples across the societal ponds, ripples that encouraged more women to step into roles of leadership and public service.

Years after her pioneering election, Mary Bellamy's legacy endures as a testament to the progress women have made in politics. In classrooms, her story is told to inspire young girls to reach for their highest aspirations. Her commitment to social issues remains relevant, echoing in the continued efforts for gender parity and social justice. Mary Bellamy's life is a reminder that every step forward paves the way for a thousand more to follow, and the baton of progress she carried is now in the hands of a new generation ready to run their leg of the race.

National Implications of Wyoming's Suffrage

During the late 19th century, the broader American political landscape was decidedly ambivalent about women's suffrage. Although other states had debated the issue, none had taken the decisive step to enfranchise women fully.

One of the earliest and most direct impacts of Wyoming's decision was the bolstering of the national suffragist movement. Suffrage advocates, who had been working tirelessly but with limited success, now had a tangible example to cite. Wyoming became a beacon, demonstrating that women's enfranchisement was possible and beneficial. Organizations like the National Woman Suffrage Association and the American Woman Suffrage Association, led by luminaries such as Susan B. Anthony and Elizabeth Cady Stanton, showcased Wyoming as proof that their cause was both just and feasible.

Wyoming's decision placed a considerable amount of pressure on other states and territories. As the rest of the nation watched, territories like Utah and Washington were influenced to grant women the right to vote during the 1870s and 1880s, although with varying levels of permanence. States in the West that often championed themselves as vanguards of progress and innovation felt the impetus to reevaluate their stance on the voting issue.

Wyoming's commitment to women's enfranchisement truly shone when it sought statehood. In 1890, as Wyoming prepared to join the Union, there was pressure from federal legislators to rescind women's suffrage to align more closely with the rest of the nation. Wyoming's response was unwavering. The territory's officials stated Wyoming would remain out of the Union for a hundred years rather than join without its women. Such staunch commitment clarified that the principles of equality were non-negotiable for Wyoming. They admitted the territory as the 44th state without compromising on its stand, further cementing its title as the "Equality State."

The influence of Wyoming's early commitment to women's suffrage cannot be overstated. It gave the national suffrage movement momentum, offering both a model and a challenge to the rest of the nation. It also played a vital role in shaping the discourse that eventually led to the ratification of the 19th Amendment.

Chapter 7 – Wyoming Becomes a State (1890)

As the 19th century ended, the vast and varied tapestry of American territories steadily transitioned into statehood, each with its own unique story. Wyoming's journey toward statehood, set against the backdrop of its rich history of indigenous cultures, pioneering settlers, and groundbreaking policies, is a testament to its resilience and visionary spirit. In 1890, this expansive land, once perceived primarily as a thoroughfare for westward expansion, would solidify its place in the Union, bringing a legacy of equality and frontier tenacity.

The transition from territory to state is never merely a change in status. It reflects a region's maturation, readiness to fully participate in the nation's governance, and affirmation of shared values and ambitions. For Wyoming, its unique challenges, aspirations, and the undeniable influence of its diverse populace shaped the path to statehood. As we delve into this pivotal period, we will explore the intricate processes, the fervent debates, and the collective hopes that culminated in Wyoming's emergence as the 44th state of the United States.

Statehood and Constitutional Development

Like many territories of its time, Wyoming's journey to statehood was a blend of socio-political maneuvers, economic aspirations, and an underlying desire for greater autonomy. However, what sets Wyoming's narrative apart is its leaders' distinctive vision for the state, made especially clear in its pioneering constitutional development.

By the late 1880s, Wyoming had witnessed a substantial increase in its non-indigenous population, driven by factors ranging from the allure of vast grazing lands to the promise of mineral riches. As population numbers grew, so did the collective sentiment for greater representation at a national level. While providing a semblance of order, the territorial governance structure often lacked the authority or resources to fully address Wyoming's unique challenges.

The initial push for statehood can be traced back to a broader national strategy, where the Republican Party, in its desire to maintain control in the Senate, was inclined to admit Republican-leaning territories as states. Wyoming's territorial legislature, dominated by Republicans, was understandably keen on this prospect. But beyond political alignments, statehood represented an opportunity for Wyoming's residents to define their future, especially through the drafting of a state constitution.

In September 1889, forty-nine delegates convened in Cheyenne for the Constitutional Convention. The diverse group was comprised of ranchers, lawyers, miners, and businessmen. Noticeably, while women had secured the right to vote in the territory, female representation in the convention was conspicuously absent. However, their influence was unmistakably present in the ensuing discussions.

The delegates faced the daunting task of crafting a foundational document that catered to Wyoming's present and remained adaptable to its unforeseeable future. They examined other state constitutions, drawing lessons from them, but also ensured that Wyoming's constitution addressed its unique circumstances.

A significant aspect of the constitution was, of course, its stance on women's rights. Beyond gender rights, the constitution delved into intricate details, from the separation of powers to guidelines on public education. It emphasized checks and balances, perhaps reflective of the territory's experiences with sometimes overbearing federal oversight. Additionally, provisions were made to ensure that the state's natural resources, which included its rich mineral deposits and grazing lands, were managed sustainably. This foresight was pivotal, as it would guide Wyoming's economic decisions well into the future.

Once the draft was finalized after rigorous discussions and debates, it was put forth for public ratification. In November 1889, Wyoming's electorate, which now notably included women, voted overwhelmingly in favor of the proposed constitution.

With a ratified constitution in hand, Wyoming's plea for statehood was formally presented to the U.S. Congress. On July 10, 1890, President Benjamin Harrison signed a statehood bill, marking Wyoming's transition from a territory to the 44th state of the Union.

Economic and Social Changes in the 20th Century

The 20th century marked a period of transformative change for Wyoming, as it did for much of the United States. However, the intricacies of Wyoming's evolution—colored by its unique geographical position, natural resources, and sociopolitical atmosphere—made its journey distinct.

Economic Transformations

The turn of the century saw Wyoming's economy, once heavily reliant on agriculture, diversify into other sectors. The state's mineral wealth, particularly coal and oil, took center stage. The discovery of oil fields in places like Salt Creek brought an influx of investment and workers. By the mid-20th century, Wyoming significantly contributed to America's energy sector. These energy resources altered the economic landscape and reshaped entire communities, with towns burgeoning around mining and drilling sites.

While minerals played a pivotal role, it would be remiss not to mention the continued importance of agriculture. The open ranges, conducive for livestock rearing, ensured that cattle ranching remained a vital part of Wyoming's identity. Over the decades, innovations in farming techniques and introduction of irrigation systems also propelled crop farming, particularly sugar beets and barley.

Social Shifts and Demographic Changes

The economic transformations brought with them significant social and demographic changes. The rise of the energy sector attracted a diverse pool of workers from within the US and abroad. Towns previously marked by homogeneity began to witness increased diversity, enriching Wyoming's cultural tapestry. This period also saw the rise of labor movements, especially in mining towns, as workers advocated for better conditions and wages.

Wyoming's stance on women's rights continued to influence social dynamics. Women actively participated in the state's economic and social spheres. Their roles weren't limited to traditional sectors but spanned newer industries like oil and gas.

Education saw a marked emphasis. The establishment of the University of Wyoming in the late 19th century was a precursor to the state's commitment to higher education. As the 20th century progressed, efforts were channeled into ensuring that quality education was accessible across the state, from its bustling towns to its more remote regions.

Impact of Global Events

The two World Wars and the Great Depression were not just distant global events; they left indelible marks on Wyoming. During the World Wars, Wyomingites served in commendable numbers. The state's mineral resources, especially oil, became crucial to the national war effort. The Great Depression, while primarily an economic downturn, had deep-seated social implications. Communities rallied together, showcasing the resilience that Wyoming has often been celebrated for. Federal initiatives, like the New Deal, played a role in mitigating some of the adverse effects, with infrastructural projects providing employment to many.

Emergence of Tourism

By the mid-20th century, Wyoming's breathtaking landscapes, previously seen primarily as resources or barriers, began to be recognized for their touristic value. National parks like Yellowstone and Grand Teton became focal points for domestic and international tourists alike. The state's rich history, encompassing tales of indigenous tribes, pioneers, and outlaws, added layers to its allure. Tourism, initially a secondary sector, began contributing significantly to the state's coffers.

The 20th century, for Wyoming, was not just about economic prosperity or challenges; it was about evolution. It was a period when the state navigated the complex maze of modernization while holding onto its foundational values. From the vast open ranches to the bustling energy towns, from the halls of academia in Laramie to the serene beauty of national parks, Wyoming's story in the 20th century is a testament to its adaptability and resilience. As the century ended, Wyoming stood poised with lessons from its rich past and aspirations for a promising future.

Chapter 8 – The Energy Frontier

Wyoming has historically been the stage for many transformative eras—from the journeys of indigenous tribes to the trails of pioneers. Yet, as the 20th century unfolded, a new chapter defined the state's identity and economic trajectory: the era of energy. The coal beds, oil reservoirs, and natural gas pockets beneath Wyoming's terrain were no longer dormant secrets but central to the state's fortunes and the nation's energy aspirations. In this chapter, we delve into Wyoming's evolution as a pivotal player in America's energy frontier, examining the challenges, triumphs, and intricate interplay between man, economy, and nature.

Oil, Natural Gas, and Coal

Wyoming stood atop three geological treasures—oil, natural gas, and coal. The extraction and utilization of these resources reshaped the state's landscape, both literally and figuratively, serving as catalysts for economic growth and introducing the broader implications of energy politics and environmental considerations.

Oil in Wyoming

For generations, the dark, glossy sheen of oil seeping through Wyoming's soil was a familiar sight to its residents. Native American tribes, using its distinctive properties for medicinal and ceremonial purposes, were well aware of the land's hidden treasure. Similarly, early settlers, while recognizing these oil seepages, were only beginning to grasp the vast potential they hinted at.

The first sale of oil recorded in history was at the hands of those along the Oregon Trail. Oil seepage found in Oil Mountain Springs, west of what's now Casper, Wyoming, was sold to travelers to oil or lubricate their wagon wheels on the long journey.

The real shift, however, began in 1884, a pivotal year in Wyoming's relationship with oil. "Mike Murphy #1" was thrust into operation, marking the birth of Wyoming's commercial oil industry. Mike Murphy, an Irishman from Pennsylvania, moved west as a land surveyor in 1854. Inspired by Washington Irving's book *The Adventures of Captain Bonneville, aka Scenes Beyond the Rocky Mountains of the Far West,* he and his brother drilled 300 feet at Captain Bonneville's "great tar spring" and struck oil. This first well did strict business with the Union Pacific Railway, which used the oil as a lubricant for railcar axles.

Over the subsequent years, the state's oil landscape transformed dramatically. Explorers and geologists, in their relentless quest for black gold, stumbled upon many fields. The Salt Creek Field, uncovered in 1908, stands out among these. Nestled in the heart of the Rocky Mountains, this field unveiled one of the largest oil reserves in the region, catapulting Wyoming into the spotlight.

By the time the Roaring Twenties rolled around, Wyoming was not just a minor oil player but an oil powerhouse. The state's annual production soared, exceeding thirty-five million barrels. Wyoming's once quiet, expansive landscapes buzzed with the sounds of drilling and machinery.

This oil boom did more than just boost production figures. Local and far-off companies, enticed by the state's prolific reserves, set their sights on Wyoming. The raw, thick crude was extracted from the earth, transported to refineries, and meticulously processed. What emerged were refined products, from gasoline to lubricants, ready to fuel a rapidly modernizing nation.

Natural Gas

In 1939, Wyoming's vast energy landscape caught the eye of the California Oil Company. Hopeful for oil, they delved into the depths beneath the state's terrain. However, instead of the coveted black gold, they unearthed natural gas. The discovery wasn't what they'd hoped for, and the well changed hands to the El Paso Gas Company. Over the next decade or so, El Paso, undeterred by the initial findings, drilled seven wells. Unfortunately, these wells didn't yield much gas, either.

There were clear challenges to accessing the gas trapped beneath the sandstone. One of the more outlandish solutions proposed was the use of nuclear devices to shatter this obstinate barrier—a plan that was met with swift resistance from the local community and was promptly shelved. The Meridian Oil Company tried their luck next, hoping for better fortune. But they, too, faced similar setbacks, with the sandstone proving a formidable opponent.

With these recurring challenges and a limited market for natural gas, the mood surrounding its extraction was one of skepticism. For a time, it seemed that Wyoming's vast natural gas reserves might remain just out of reach. However, the landscape changed dramatically with the Clean Air Act of 1970. This landmark legislation spurred a renewed interest in cleaner energy sources, and natural gas was back in the spotlight.

Enter the McMurry Oil Company. Based in Casper, Wyoming, this forward-thinking company saw the potential of natural gas as a clean-burning energy source. While the Environmental Protection Agency would later raise concerns about natural gas emissions, it was a promising alternative to more polluting fuels at that time. Moreover, the initial low natural gas prices meant drilling leases were a bargain. Seizing this opportunity, McMurry Oil acquired three wells in the Jonah Field in 1991, along with mineral leases spanning 25,000 acres of land governed by the Bureau of Land Management.

Initial tests were promising. These wells could produce an impressive two million cubic feet of gas daily. However, the same old challenge persisted—the sandstone formations. The drilling process itself was compromising these structures, hampering the flow of gas.

To overcome this hurdle, the industry turned to a groundbreaking technique: hydraulic fracturing, or "fracking." The gas in these fields lay imprisoned beneath rock formations. Once a well was drilled, these rocky barriers had to be tackled. Fracking involves pumping fluids or compressed gases with immense force into these wells. The pressure creates fractures in the rock, paving pathways for the gas to flow freely. This innovative method was the key to unlocking Wyoming's vast natural gas reserves, reshaping the state's energy landscape for decades.

Coal

Wyoming's coal history stretches back to the mid-19th century, with the earliest documented discovery of coal deposits in the state dating to 1843. This discovery was made during the second Fremont Expedition, an exploratory journey to find routes to Oregon. As the expedition meandered through Wyoming in August of that year, members noted coal seams exposed in small gaps amid the hills. Six decades later, this very spot would transform into the coal camp of Cumberland, located in today's Lincoln County, Wyoming.

Such coal camps were a distinctive feature of the Rocky Mountains during that era. Entire towns sprang up around coal mining operations, and these communities were typically owned lock, stock, and barrel by the coal companies. Everything bore the imprint of the coal company from the general store where families bought their daily needs to schools where children were educated, public halls for gatherings, and even the houses where workers and their families resided.

In 1859, another notable expedition, the Raynolds Expedition, ventured into Wyoming and recorded locations of coal veins. Their observations spotlighted the Powder River Basin, which, unbeknownst to them then, would emerge as one of the nation's most significant coal fields.

Fast forward to 1867, and the landscape of Wyoming began to change significantly with the arrival of the Union Pacific Railroad. This opened doors for establishing the state's first commercial coal mining ventures. Dominating these initial mining endeavors was the Wyoming Coal and Mining Company, which leased lands directly from the railroad for their operations. However, the company's fortunes were intertwined with the railroad. When the Union Pacific decided to relocate in 1899, it spelled doom for these mines. By 1903, they had to shutter their operations. This year also witnessed a grim chapter in Wyoming's coal mining history, with an explosion in the Carbon camp leading to the tragic death of 169 miners. Today, Carbon is a haunting ghost town, with a cemetery bearing silent testimony to that tragic day.

While coal mining continued in various pockets of Wyoming, the industry gradually declined. By the 1960s, many mines were closing their doors as the energy industry's attention shifted increasingly toward oil and natural gas. Today, Wyoming's coal legacy is a blend of historical records, ghost towns, and memories of a once-thriving industry that powered the state's growth.

Boom and Bust Cycles

With its rich tap of resources, Wyoming has experienced economic rhythms mimicking the global demand for energy. These rhythms—rapid crescendos of prosperity followed by melancholic downturns—have defined much of Wyoming's modern history. The state's reliance on oil, natural gas, and coal has made it particularly susceptible to the volatile nature of global energy markets, resulting in periodic boom and bust cycles.

The Early Booms

The late 19th and early 20th centuries ushered in Wyoming's initial energy booms. For example, as mentioned, the Salt Creek Oil Field produced a record 35 million barrels of oil in 1923. The promise of jobs and wealth attracted droves of laborers and entrepreneurs to the state.

Boomtowns sprouted around major discoveries, drawing in a mosaic of workers, entrepreneurs, and families seeking to tap into the state's burgeoning energy wealth. New businesses, schools, and amenities sprouted seemingly overnight. These boom periods were characterized by rapid infrastructural development, increased population, and a sense of unbridled optimism.

While these booms brought prosperity, they also introduced social and infrastructural strains. Towns like Casper and Gillette, which once existed on the periphery of the state's consciousness, were thrust into the limelight, grappling with rapid growth and the intricacies of an economy tethered to global energy prices.

Federal interference made it harder for companies to gain the mineral rights to the land since they now had to lease it from the government instead of staking claims, as with gold, but that didn't make the energy business any less productive.

The Downturns

As history would repeatedly show, what goes up must come down. By the mid-20th century, Wyoming had experienced its fair share of downturns. These bust periods, often triggered by external factors such as global market fluctuations, decreased demand, or technological shifts, led to job losses and economic contractions.

By the late 1920s, no more oil wells were being drilled. With thousands of wells already drilled, the pressure that made the oil come to the surface for collection dissipated. More wells needed expensive pumps to collect the oil, and workers moved on to greener oil pastures in Texas and Montana. The stock market's tumultuous descent in October 1929 wasn't just a moment in history books; it was a chilling reality that gripped the nation. The subsequent Great Depression tightened its vice-like grip on the dreams and aspirations of countless families. In Wyoming, the echoes of Wall Street's crash reverberated through the oil fields. With market prices plummeting to a heart-wrenching nineteen cents per barrel, the state's heartbeat of oil production slowed drastically. By the following year, Wyoming's oil wells were drawing up merely ten million barrels annually—a stark contrast to the flourishing output that had marked the decade's onset.

For residents, the bust cycles were periods of uncertainty. The once-thriving towns witnessed dwindling populations as workers sought opportunities elsewhere. Local businesses, many of which had flourished during the boom periods, faced closures or significant cutbacks. These downturns also strained Wyoming's state budget, which relied heavily on revenue from the energy sector.

Navigating the Cycles

Wyoming's leadership, recognizing the inherent challenges of an economy tethered to global energy markets, sought to navigate these cycles with a mix of pragmatism and foresight. They tried to diversify the state's economy by investing in sectors like tourism, agriculture, and technology. The state also established a "rainy day" fund, setting aside portions of revenue during boom periods to buffer against future economic downturns.

The state focused on education and workforce training. Recognizing that a diversified skill set was crucial for resilience, institutions like the University of Wyoming and community colleges expanded their offerings, preparing residents for a broader range of career opportunities.

Environmental and Social Impacts

The boom and bust cycles had environmental and social implications. Rapid development during boom periods sometimes outpaced the environmental safeguards, leading to concerns about land degradation, water quality, and habitat disruption. Collaborating with environmental groups and industry stakeholders, the state worked towards more sustainable practices, recognizing that Wyoming's natural beauty was as much a resource as its mineral wealth.

Socially, the cycles often exacerbated existing divides. During boom periods, newcomers, drawn by the promise of jobs, sometimes found themselves at odds with long-term residents, leading to tensions over cultural and community identity. Conversely, during bust periods, communities grappled with the challenges of outmigration, with many young residents seeking opportunities outside Wyoming.

The boom and bust cycles of Wyoming's energy sector serve as a sad reminder of the state's intricate dance with global markets. These cycles, while challenging, have also been instrumental in shaping Wyoming's identity. The challenges have only increased the state's fight for resilience, adaptability, and community solidarity. As the state looks to the future, its history offers valuable lessons on navigating the ebbs and flows of economic fortune, emphasizing the importance of diversification, forward-thinking, and a deep-seated commitment to its people and the land.

The Environmental Concerns of Mineral Extraction

Wyoming's energy trajectory, much like the rest of the nation's, has been linked directly with significant environmental concerns. Balancing the quest for energy resources with environmental stewardship has been a central challenge for the state throughout the 20th century. As Wyoming capitalized on its rich mineral and fossil fuel deposits, the repercussions on the land, water, and air became progressively evident.

Impact on Landscapes

By their nature, the extraction industries lead to alterations in the natural landscape. Open-pit coal mines, drilling platforms, and expansive networks of roads and pipelines have reshaped Wyoming's terrain. In addition to the immediate physical changes, there were often secondary effects. Soil erosion, alteration of drainage patterns, and habitat disruption for wildlife emerged as prominent concerns. The vast prairies, home to pronghorns, elk, and numerous bird species, faced fragmentation, often hindering traditional migration routes and breeding grounds.

Water Quality and Availability

Water, the lifeblood of Wyoming's agricultural sector, faced challenges in terms of quality and quantity. The extraction processes, especially in the earlier days of the energy industry, were not always efficient in preventing contamination. Instances of groundwater contamination due to leakages or mismanagement of waste were reported. Additionally, the extraction processes, particularly for coal and oil, are water-intensive. This increased demand exerted pressure on Wyoming's water resources, leading to concerns about sustainable usage and long-term availability.

Air Quality

With industrial growth came increased emissions. While Wyoming's vast open spaces often dilute pollutants more effectively than congested urban areas, there were undeniable impacts on air quality. Emissions from refineries, coupled with burning fossil fuels, introduced a range of pollutants into the atmosphere.

Addressing the Concerns

As awareness of these environmental impacts grew, both public and private sectors in Wyoming took steps to address them. With an increased understanding of the detrimental effects of certain emissions on health and the environment, there was a push for stricter regulations and the adoption of cleaner technologies. Regulatory frameworks were established to balance economic growth and environmental preservation. Rigorous impact assessments became a staple before the initiation of new projects. Rehabilitation and reclamation of lands post-extraction became more systematic, with an emphasis on restoring habitats and preventing long-term damage.

Wyoming also saw the rise of environmental advocacy groups, which played an instrumental role in highlighting concerns, championing conservation causes, and working collaboratively with industries and regulators to find sustainable solutions.

Innovation and Forward Thinking

By the latter part of the 20th century, there was a notable shift towards seeking more sustainable methods of energy extraction and consumption. Technological innovations aimed at reducing emissions, minimizing waste, and ensuring efficient use of resources were increasingly integrated into Wyoming's energy landscape. Research institutions in the state began delving deeper into environmental science, providing valuable insights and innovations to reduce the environmental footprint of energy extraction.

The environmental concerns associated with Wyoming's energy endeavors underscore the intricate relationship between progress and preservation. They serve as a reminder of the state's responsibility to its vast natural treasures even as it seeks to harness its underground riches. As Wyoming continues its energy journey, the lessons from the 20th century offer valuable guidance—emphasizing the importance of proactive measures, community engagement, and a commitment to harmonizing economic aspirations with environmental imperatives.

Wyoming's energy sectors have consistently showcased adaptability. As global dynamics shifted and environmental concerns became more pronounced, Wyoming's energy industries, working with academic and research institutions, sought innovative methods to enhance extraction efficiency, reduce environmental impact, and diversify energy resources. Efforts to harness wind energy and explore the potential of carbon capture and storage underlined the state's forward-thinking approach.

National Implications

Wyoming's prominence in energy production had multifaceted national implications. On an economic front, the state's energy resources drove job creation, infrastructure development, and fiscal growth within its borders and in regions dependent on its energy exports. As a reliable energy supplier, Wyoming bolstered national energy security, reducing dependence on foreign sources.

However, it wasn't just about economics. Wyoming's decisions around energy regulation, production standards, and environmental policies often served as benchmarks for other states. The challenges faced by Wyoming, be it in water use, land reclamation, or air quality, provided valuable lessons for other energy-rich regions.

Wyoming's role in the 20th-century energy industry of the United States is undeniably significant. Beyond the sheer volume of resources it provided, the state's journey offers insights into the complexities of energy production in a changing world. Balancing economic aspirations with environmental and social considerations, Wyoming's story is a testament to the multifaceted nature of energy—both a resource and a responsibility. As the nation looks to the future of energy, the lessons from Wyoming's past and present will undoubtedly illuminate the path forward.

Chapter 9 – Modern Wyoming (Late 20th Century to Present)

As the 20th century waned, Wyoming stood on the precipice of a significant transformation. Steeped in a rich history of pioneering spirit, territorial changes, and resource-driven economies, the state faced new challenges and opportunities in the modern era. This chapter delves into Wyoming's journey from the late 20th century to the present day, chronicling its evolution in technology, social dynamics, politics, and environmental stewardship.

While the past chapters have explored the foundational elements that shaped Wyoming's identity, this chapter focuses on understanding how these elements interact with contemporary global trends. From the rise of digital innovation and the shift in energy paradigms to the evolving socio-cultural fabric of its communities, modern Wyoming emerges as a fascinating blend of tradition and change.

In the next sections, we'll dive into Wyoming's recent history, looking at the big events and stories that have shaped it. We'll give you a full picture of a state that's always changing but stays true to its roots.

Economic Diversification

In the past few decades, Wyoming's economy has been changing. While the state has a long history with industries like mining, farming, and energy, it's started to branch out. This shift comes as these industries run into new challenges, from changing market demands to new rules about the environment.

One of Wyoming's first steps towards diversification was investing in technology and innovation. Tech parks and innovation hubs began emerging in cities like Cheyenne and Casper. These establishments aimed to attract startups and tech firms and foster a culture of entrepreneurship among the youth. The University of Wyoming played a pivotal role, offering programs that emphasized tech-driven careers and establishing research centers that foster innovation.

Another significant shift was the push towards tourism. While Wyoming had always been a haven for nature lovers, thanks to its expansive national parks and captivating landscapes, a concerted effort was made to brand the state as a premier tourist destination. Events, festivals, and marketing campaigns highlighted its diverse offerings—from winter sports in Jackson Hole to the historic allure of places like Cody. The growth of eco-tourism, which emphasized sustainable travel to natural areas, also played to Wyoming's strengths, with its unspoiled wilderness and commitment to conservation.

Agriculture, a mainstay of Wyoming's economy, also underwent a transformation. As global markets evolved, there was a push to shift from traditional farming to more niche markets. Organic farming, specialty livestock breeding, and farm-to-table initiatives gained traction. Wyoming's beef, in particular, found its way to international markets, benefiting from branding that emphasized its quality and organic nature.

Economic diversification didn't mean a complete move away from energy. Instead, the focus shifted to sustainable energy solutions. The vast open landscapes of Wyoming proved conducive for wind and solar energy farms. Several projects were initiated to harness these renewable sources, with the state government offering incentives for sustainable energy ventures.

But challenges persisted. As with any transition, there were sectors that faced downturns and communities that had to adjust to new realities. Some towns, historically reliant on coal mining, grappled with unemployment and a changing demographic as younger residents moved to urban centers or out of state seeking diverse opportunities.

Nevertheless, the overall push for economic diversification showcased Wyoming's adaptability. While honoring its rich history and traditions, the state displayed readiness to embrace change, ensuring its economic vitality in the modern era. By striking a balance between innovation and tradition, Wyoming positioned itself as a state that could navigate the complexities of the global economy while staying true to its roots.

Cultural and Social Developments

As Wyoming navigated the economic transitions of the late 20th and early 21st centuries, it concurrently witnessed a rich tapestry of cultural and social developments. While influenced by national and global trends, these shifts bore a distinct Wyoming character, shaped by its landscapes, history, and resilient spirit.

Starting with the arts, Wyoming underwent a renaissance. Casper, Laramie, and Cheyenne became bustling centers of artistic expression. Local galleries began displaying works from artists inspired by Wyoming's landscapes and cultural heritage. These weren't just traditional Western scenes, either; contemporary artists melded the old with the new, producing pieces that evoked Wyoming's past while hinting at its future. Additionally, art festivals, like the annual Wyoming Arts Summit, provided platforms for artists to connect, collaborate, and showcase their work, drawing visitors from around the nation.

Literature and writing experienced a boom, as well. Wyoming's landscapes, history, and evolving identity became the backdrop for novels, poetry, and nonfiction. Local writers' workshops and festivals, such as the Jackson Hole Writers Conference, facilitated a space for budding and seasoned writers alike. These gatherings emphasized storytelling that was both universal and deeply rooted in Wyoming's experiences.

In the realm of music, while country and folk remained beloved, there was a noticeable diversification in the musical scene. Music festivals featuring genres ranging from jazz to rock to bluegrass became annual events in the state's calendar. Wyoming also produced a new generation of musicians who, while influenced by the state's musical heritage, were keen on experimenting and branching into diverse genres.

Socially, Wyoming, like much of America, faced debates and introspection on issues like LGBTQ+ rights, immigration, and racial justice. The state's traditionally conservative ethos was sometimes in dialogue and sometimes in tension with progressive viewpoints. Communities across the state hosted forums and discussions, with many Wyomingites emphasizing the importance of understanding and unity. Schools and colleges became hubs for activism and discourse, with younger generations significantly shaping these conversations.

Another notable social shift was the emphasis on preserving Wyoming's indigenous cultures. The state saw a resurgence of interest in its Native American heritage, with efforts to integrate indigenous histories and perspectives into school curriculums. Events celebrating Native cultures, traditions, and arts gained prominence, fostering a deeper appreciation and understanding among residents.

However, with these developments came challenges. As Wyoming opened itself up to the world and embraced modernity, there were concerns about the erosion of its distinct identity. Debates raged over what it meant to be a Wyomingite in the modern era. While some argued for holding onto traditional values, others contended that change was inevitable and should be embraced.

Despite these challenges, Wyoming managed to carve a niche for itself. By the turn of the 21st century, it wasn't just seen as a state of ranchers and miners but as a haven for artists, writers, musicians, and thinkers. Its ability to hold onto its traditions while being receptive to change became its greatest strength.

The cultural and social developments in Wyoming during the late 20th and early 21st centuries were a testament to its evolving identity. Through its art, music, literature, and social discourse, Wyoming displayed its ability to respect its past while looking confidently toward the future.

Political Landscape

The late 20th century and the dawn of the 21st century were dynamic periods for Wyoming's political landscape, marked by both continuity and change. As one of the least populous states, Wyoming's politics often displayed an intimate character, deeply connected to its people and their experiences.

One of the most consistent elements of Wyoming's politics has been its conservative leanings. The Republican Party held significant sway in the state, often securing gubernatorial, congressional, and local seats. This political orientation was tied to Wyoming's rugged individualism, its economic reliance on industries like energy and agriculture, and its rural nature.

However, beneath this overarching conservative banner, nuances were evident. In urban centers like Cheyenne and Laramie, there was a noticeable liberal presence, reflective of younger demographics and university communities. These areas became the nexus for debates on environmental policies, LGBTQ+ rights, and education reforms.

Though small, Wyoming's representation in Washington, D.C., was influential. Senators and representatives from the state frequently played crucial roles in energy, environmental, and land use policy discussions. Their positions often reflected the state's interests, emphasizing both the economic importance of resource industries and the significance of preserving Wyoming's natural beauty.

An intriguing facet of Wyoming's political scene was the participation of women. Remembered as the "Equality State," Wyoming had a history of being ahead of the curve in women's rights. This legacy translated into the modern era, with women actively taking part and holding office at various governmental levels. Their influence underscores Wyoming's unique blend of traditional values and progressive stances.

New political discussions emerged in response to the economic diversifications and changing social fabric. The balance between economic growth and environmental preservation became a recurrent theme. As the state's economy ventured beyond traditional sectors, debates on regulatory measures, incentives for emerging industries, and workforce education gained prominence.

A commendable trait of Wyoming's politics was its emphasis on public engagement. Town hall meetings, community forums, and public consultations were common, allowing residents to have a say in shaping policies. This participatory approach symbolized Wyoming's ethos—a state proud of its roots yet adaptive to the times.

Governance presented both challenges and opportunities. As the state underwent transformations in various spheres, its governance structures had to adapt to be more responsive. The devolution of certain powers to local bodies, increased public participation in decision-making, and transparency in governance were seen as potential avenues to achieve this.

Wyoming's political landscape at the turn of the 21st century was a mosaic of tradition and modernity. While it kept its foundational conservative core, it wasn't resistant to change, reflecting its people's evolving aspirations and concerns.

Challenges and Opportunities

At the nexus of the late 20th century and the onset of the 21st, Wyoming found itself in a transformative phase. With its rich history as a backdrop, the state faced both multifaceted challenges and promising opportunities that would determine its future trajectory.

Cultural preservation and evolution coexisted as intertwined themes. While it was essential to honor Wyoming's rich heritage, there was also a need to embrace the changing cultural fabric brought about by migration, technology, and global influences. Celebrating diversity, acknowledging the contributions of indigenous communities, and fostering a sense of inclusivity became more than just ideals; they were necessities for a harmonious society.

In hindsight, this period was emblematic of Wyoming's spirit. Though grounded in its historical roots, the state displayed resilience, adaptability, and foresight. By recognizing challenges as avenues for growth and capitalizing on inherent opportunities, Wyoming sought to carve a path that was both respectful of its past and hopeful for its future.

Chapter 10 – Wyoming's Natural Beauty and Conservation Efforts

Wyoming, a state often synonymous with vast open spaces, majestic peaks, and untouched landscapes, offers a visual testament to nature's grandeur. From the whispering prairies of the east to the formidable Rocky Mountains in the west, Wyoming's topography tells a tale of geologic wonders and the ceaseless dance of flora and fauna. But beyond the breathtaking vistas lies a story of conscious stewardship, of generations that recognized the state's unique gifts and endeavored to preserve them for the ages. In this chapter, we delve into the intrinsic beauty of Wyoming's natural assets and trace the state's journey in conserving these treasures, understanding how the interplay between appreciation and preservation has shaped its legacy.

National Parks and Protected Areas

Wyoming's diverse landscapes, encompassing everything from sweeping plains to towering mountain ranges, have been recognized and safeguarded through a network of national parks and protected areas. These areas aren't just vacation spots for countless visitors every year; they're vital safe zones for unique ecosystems and many animals.

Yellowstone National Park, set up in 1872, has the honor of being the first national park in the world. It stretches across parts of Montana, Idaho, and Wyoming. It's known for its volcanic activity—think geysers and hot springs—but it's also home to a wide range of wildlife. If you're lucky, you might spot bison, wolves, or even grizzlies living free in the park.

Moving south, **Grand Teton National Park** paints a contrasting picture. Identified by the jagged peaks of the Teton Range, this park's landscape merges alpine lakes, dense forests, and pristine rivers. Unlike its northern counterpart, Grand Teton offers a more intimate connection with the mountainous terrain, inviting climbers, hikers, and nature lovers to immerse themselves in its beautiful but treacherous nature.

Besides the eminent national parks, Wyoming boasts a myriad of national monuments, forests, and wildlife refuges. **Devil's Tower National Monument,** mentioned previously, is an arresting geologic formation rising dramatically from the northeastern plains. It is revered by several Native American tribes and draws both cultural and rock-climbing enthusiasts. Meanwhile, the **Bighorn Canyon National Recreation Area** exhibits the might of the Bighorn River, which has sculpted dramatic red cliffs and deep canyons into the landscape.

The state's commitment to ecological preservation is also evident in its national forests. The Bridger-Teton National Forest and Shoshone National Forest, among others, contribute vast swathes of protected woodland, offering habitats for wildlife and recreation for humans. These woodlands, intertwined with trails and interspersed with alpine meadows and lakes, represent Wyoming's dedication to conserving its diverse landscapes.

Equally vital in this conservation matrix are the wildlife refuges. Places like the Seedskadee National Wildlife Refuge prioritize the protection of bird habitats, ensuring that both migratory and resident species have safe havens. These refuges, often less frequented by the public, play a silent but crucial role in maintaining the ecological balance of the state.

Wyoming's national parks and protected areas are more than just scenic destinations. They are the state's pledge to future generations, a testament to the belief that nature in its undisturbed state is invaluable. Through deliberate measures, collaborative efforts, and an enduring appreciation of the land, Wyoming continues its legacy as a steward of America's unparalleled natural beauty.

Wildlife Conservation

Wyoming's land is a mix of open plains and rugged terrains, and it is home to a variety of wildlife. Bison can be seen grazing, and golden eagles fly overhead. The state values these animals as symbols and essential parts of the ecosystem. With habitats everywhere under pressure, Wyoming's efforts to protect its wildlife are more important than ever.

A big player in these efforts is the Wyoming Game and Fish Department (WGFD). Set up in the early 1900s, it's the go-to agency for managing Wyoming's fish and wildlife. The WGFD studies animals, repairs habitats, and teaches the public about wildlife. Its goal is to make sure nature keeps thriving in Wyoming, even as towns and cities grow.

One of the chief points for Wyoming's conservation work has been bringing back the gray wolf. These wolves were nearly gone from most of the US. But with hard work, including reintroducing them and setting up protections, gray wolves are now back in the Greater Yellowstone Ecosystem. Now, if you're in the right spot in Wyoming, you might hear a wolf's howl echoing in the distance. Another iconic species, the grizzly bear, has similarly benefited from targeted conservation initiatives. The grizzly population, having faced precipitous declines in the past, is now cautiously rebounding thanks to robust monitoring and habitat management programs.

But it's not just the charismatic megafauna that benefit from Wyoming's conservation mindset. Lesser-known species, from the sage grouse with its intricate mating dance to the cutthroat trout, a native of Wyoming's freshwater systems, are subjects of dedicated research and protection measures. This holistic approach ensures that every cog in the ecological machine receives due attention.

Collaboration has been the bedrock of Wyoming's wildlife conservation efforts. Ranchers, environmentalists, Native American tribes, and federal agencies often set aside their differences and come together, driven by a shared reverence for the state's natural inhabitants. This spirit of cooperation has led to the preservation of species and ensured that the local communities remain invested in and benefit from conservation.

Wyoming's approach to wildlife conservation stands as a beacon for others to emulate. By striking a harmonious balance between development and protection and fostering collaboration among various stakeholders, the state has ensured that its rich tapestry of wildlife continues to flourish for generations to come.

Recreation and Tourism

With its soul-stirring expanses and raw natural elegance, Wyoming has always whispered promises of adventure to those with wanderlust. Its landscape, a rich tapestry of snow-draped mountains, gentle grasslands, and hidden valleys, paints a picture that's been captivating souls for ages, weaving itself deeply into Wyoming's economic and cultural story.

When the 20th century dawned and introduced the idea of national parks, Wyoming's whispered promises became a clarion call for nature lovers everywhere. At the forefront, Yellowstone stood proudly, wearing the badge of America's first national park. It invited travelers to lose themselves in its geysers and the silent tales of its vast, untamed stretches. Meanwhile, the stoic peaks and mirror-like waters of Grand Teton National Park whispered their own tales of age-old legends and timeless beauty. These natural havens, each with its unique charm, became the heartbeat of Wyoming's natural landscape, welcoming millions of visitors year after year.

Yet, the state's recreational offerings are not limited to national parks. State parks, forests, and public lands present a vast array of activities. Fly-fishing enthusiasts find solace in the meandering rivers and streams, while hikers and bikers have thousands of trails at their disposal, each offering unique vistas and challenges.

Winter transforms Wyoming into a snowy paradise, with ski resorts like Jackson Hole becoming hotspots for both seasoned professionals and novices. The state's expansive wilderness areas also provide opportunities for snowshoeing, cross-country skiing, and snowmobiling, ensuring a full slate of activities for those visiting in the colder months.

Tourism, borne out of this rich recreational landscape, has significantly bolstered Wyoming's economy. Towns such as Cody, with its renowned Buffalo Bill Center of the West, and Sheridan, known for its vibrant arts scene and historic downtown, have grown and revitalized. These towns and many like them serve as gateways to Wyoming's natural wonders while offering a taste of the state's rich history and culture.

Crucially, Wyoming has recognized the need to balance tourism with conservation. Sustainable practices are emphasized, ensuring that the attractions drawing visitors remain unspoiled for future generations. This commitment is evident in the well-maintained trails, visitor education programs, and ongoing conservation initiatives throughout the state.

In essence, recreation and tourism in Wyoming are more than mere economic drivers. They represent a marriage of the state's awe-inspiring natural assets with its cultural heritage, fostering a deep appreciation for both among residents and visitors alike.

Balancing Development with Conservation

Wyoming's history is a practical story of balancing resource use with preservation. The state has rich mineral deposits but is also home to some of the country's most untouched landscapes.

During the late 1800s and early 1900s, there was a push to mine coal, drill for oil, and tap natural gas, all of which shaped Wyoming's economy. But even as these industries grew, there was a clear understanding of the importance of protecting the environment. This led to the creation of national parks and protected areas.

Today, Wyoming is at a crossroads. There's a lot of money to be made from its natural resources, but there's also a growing awareness of the value of conservation, not just for the environment but for industries like tourism. The challenge is finding the right balance.

In response, Wyoming has pioneered efforts to strike this balance. Rigorous environmental assessments, stakeholder consultations, and sustainable practices have become standard. Meanwhile, investments in renewable energy signal a forward-looking approach. Wyoming's story is one of equilibrium, where the drive for progress coexists with an unwavering commitment to protecting its natural legacy for generations to come.

Conclusion

From its earliest indigenous inhabitants to the contemporary era, Wyoming's history is richly woven with transformative events and powerful narratives. The westward expansion, epitomized by the Oregon Trail, showcased the state's position as a crossroads, while the establishment of vital outposts underscored its strategic significance. The Mormon Pioneer Trail added layers of religious and cultural nuance, while the fate of indigenous communities bore witness to the sweeping tide of change.

The late 19th century brought a series of groundbreaking events. From the cattle boom to the consequential Johnson County War, economic aspirations often clashed with existing social structures. As Wyoming moved towards statehood in 1890, it made a pioneering stride in gender equality by being the first to grant women the right to vote.

The 20th century saw Wyoming evolve as an energy frontier, with oil, gas, and coal driving its economy. But with these booms came inevitable busts, leading to a reflection on sustainability and environmental responsibility. The latter part of the century and the early 21st has been characterized by economic diversification, cultural enrichment, and political evolution, with a keen eye on balancing growth with conservation.

Wyoming's narrative is not just a regional story; it's fundamentally American. As the "Equality State," Wyoming shattered gender norms and set a precedent for the nation. Its landscapes, from Yellowstone to the Grand Tetons, have become emblematic of the American wilderness ideal. Its energy resources have powered the nation's growth, and its ranches and rodeos have epitomized the romantic vision of the American West.

But more than these, Wyoming's history is a testament to the American spirit of resilience, innovation, and adaptability. In its challenges and triumphs, we can trace the larger trajectory of a nation expanding westward, grappling with its identity, and continuously reinventing itself.

Looking ahead, Wyoming stands at a pivotal juncture. The challenges of the 21st century—climate change, economic shifts, and social transformations—are not unique to the state, but how Wyoming responds will define its future. The ongoing balance between energy production and environmental stewardship will be crucial. As technology reshapes industries, Wyoming's adaptability will be tested.

Yet, history has shown that Wyoming possesses an indomitable spirit. Rooted in its rich past and informed by its challenges, the state is poised to craft a future that honors its heritage while forging a sustainable and inclusive path forward.

Here's another book by Captivating History that you might like

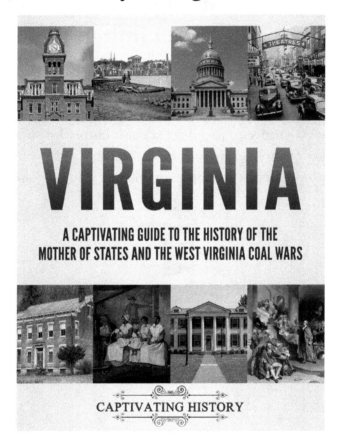

Free Bonus from Captivating History (Available for a Limited time)

Hi History Lovers!

Now you have a chance to join our exclusive history list so you can get your first history ebook for free as well as discounts and a potential to get more history books for free! Simply visit the link below to join.

Captivatinghistory.com/ebook

Also, make sure to follow us on Facebook, Twitter and Youtube by searching for Captivating History.

References

Chapter 1

"Research Confirms Eastern Wyoming Paleoindian Site as Americas Oldest Mine" https://www.uwyo.edu/news/2022/05/research-confirms-eastern-wyoming-paleoindian-site-as-americas-oldest-mine.html Accessed: September 2, 2023.

"Yellowstone Paleoindian Period: 12,000 to 8,000 years before present" https://www.nps.gov/yell/learn/historyculture/archeologypaleo.htm Accessed: September 2, 2023.

"Finley Bison Kill Site" https://www.wyohistory.org/encyclopedia/finley-bison-kill-site Accessed: September 2, 2023.

"Ancient America: Wyoming Before 6000 BCE" http://nativeamericannetroots.net/diary/1991 Accessed: September 2, 2023.

"The Prehistoric Peoples of Jackson Hole" http://www.npshistory.com/publications/grte/hrs/chap2.htm Accessed: September 2, 2023.

Toom, Dennis L. Toom (August 2004). "Northeastern Plains Village Complex Timelines and Relations." *Plains Anthropologist.* **49** (191): 281.

"The Plains Indians" https://www.nps.gov/articles/000/the-plains-indians.htm Accessed: September 2, 2023.

Bamforth, Douglas B. *The Archaeology of the North American Great Plains.* Cambridge University Press, 2021.

"Plains Woodland" https://coloradoencyclopedia.org/article/plains-woodland Accessed: September 2, 2023.

"A Place of Reverence for Native Americans"
https://www.nps.gov/deto/learn/historyculture/reverence.htm Accessed:
September 3, 2023.

Chapter 2

"Historical Timeline of Wyoming" https://www.legendsofamerica.com/wy-timeline/#:~:text=1807%2D1808%20%E2%80%93%20Fresh%20from%20the,written%20reports%20%E2%80%9CColter's%20Hell.%E2%80%9D Accessed:
September 3, 2023.

"Verendrye Family"
http://plainshumanities.unl.edu/encyclopedia/doc/egp.ea.039 Accessed:
September 4, 2023.

Smith, G. Hubert, 1980. "Explorations of the La Verendryes in the Northern
Plains, 1738-43." Lincoln: University of Nebraska Press.

"Wyoming and the Louisiana Purchase" http://wyoming-fact-and-fiction.blogspot.com/2016/02/wyoming-and-louisiana-purchase.html Accessed:
September 5, 2023.

"The Senate Approves for Ratification the Louisiana Purchase Treaty"
https://www.senate.gov/about/powers-procedures/treaties/senate-approves-louisiana-purchase-treaty.htm Accessed: September 5, 2023.

"The Fur Trade in Wyoming" https://www.wyohistory.org/encyclopedia/fur-trade-wyoming Accessed: September 6, 2023.

"Was John Colter the First White Man to Travel Through Yellowstone?"
https://www.yellowstonepark.com/park/history/john-colter-yellowstone-explorer/ Accessed: September 6, 2023.

Chapter 3

"Oregon Trail" https://www.wyohistory.org/travel/oregon-trail Accessed:
September 7, 2023.

"The Oregon-California Trail Across Wyoming"
https://www.legendsofamerica.com/wy-orgcaltrail/ Accessed: September 7,
2023.

"Basic Facts About the Oregon Trail"
https://web.archive.org/web/20160304084450/http://www.blm.gov/or/oregontrail/history-basics.php Accessed: September 7, 2023.

"Mormon Pioneer"
http://npshistory.com/publications/mopi/index.htm#:~:text=From%201846%20to%201869%20more,Great%20Salt%20Lake%20in%20Utah. Accessed:
September 7, 2023.

"The Martin's Cove Controversy" https://www.wyohistory.org/encyclopedia/martins-cove-controversy Accessed: September 8, 2023.

"Donner and Reed Wagon Train Incident" https://www.nps.gov/cali/learn/historyculture/donner-reed-party.htm Accessed: September 9, 2023.

"Narcissa Whitman" https://www.nps.gov/oreg/learn/historyculture/narcissa-whitman.htm Accessed: September 9, 2023.

"Ezra Meeker – Oregon Trail Pioneer" https://www.legendsofamerica.com/ezra-meeker/ Accessed: September 9, 2023.

"The Grattan Fight – Prelude to a Generation of War" https://www.wyohistory.org/encyclopedia/grattan-fight-prelude-generation-war Accessed: September 9, 2023.

"The Grattan Massacre" http://npshistory.com/publications/fola/nh-v37-1956.pdf Accessed: September 9, 2023.

"Sand Creek Massacre" https://www.nps.gov/sand/learn/historyculture/massacre.htm#:~:text=On%20N ovember%2029%2C%201864%2C%20675,dead%20were%20women%20and% 20children. Accessed: September 9, 2023.

"Red Cloud's War" https://www.wyohistory.org/encyclopedia/red-clouds-war Accessed: September 9, 2023.

"Flight of the Nez Perce" https://www.nps.gov/yell/learn/historyculture/flightnezperce.htm Accessed: September 9, 2023.

Chapter 4

"Formation of the Oregon Territory" https://www.nps.gov/places/formation-of-the-oregon-territory.htm Accessed: September 10, 2023.

"Treaty of Fort Laramie 1868" https://www.archives.gov/milestone-documents/fort-laramie-treaty Accessed: September 10, 2023.

"Fort Laramie Treaty of 1851 (Horse Creek Treaty)" https://www.nps.gov/articles/000/horse-creek-treaty.htm Accessed: September 10, 2023.

"In 1868, Two Nations Made a Treaty, the U.S. Broke it and Plains Indian Tribes are Still Seeking Justice" https://www.smithsonianmag.com/smithsonian-institution/1868-two-nations-made-treaty-us-broke-it-and-plains-indian-tribes-are-still-seeking-justice-180970741/ Accessed: September 10, 2023.

"South Pass Gold Rush" https://www.wyohistory.org/encyclopedia/south-pass-gold-rush Accessed: September 10, 2023.

"Miner's Delight, Wyoming" https://www.legendsofamerica.com/wy-minersdelight/ Accessed: September 10, 2023.

"Congress creates Wyoming Territory, July 25, 1868" https://www.politico.com/story/2018/07/25/this-day-in-politics-july-25-1868-734494 Accessed: September 10, 2023.

"Building the Union Pacific Railroad" https://www.wyominghistoryday.org/theme-topics/building-union-pacific-railroad#:~:text=Track%20laying%20continued%20across%20Wyoming,%2C%20on%20May%2010%2C%201869. Accessed: September 10, 2023.

"Industry, Politics, and Power: the Union Pacific in Wyoming" https://www.wyohistory.org/encyclopedia/industry-politics-and-power-union-pacific-wyoming Accessed: September 10, 2023.

Chapter 5

"The Wyoming Cattle Boom, 1868-1886" https://www.wyohistory.org/encyclopedia/wyoming-cattle-boom-1868-1886 Accessed: September 12, 2023.

"The Johnson County War: 1892 Invasion of Northern Wyoming" https://www.wyohistory.org/encyclopedia/johnson-county-war-1892-invasion-northern-wyoming Accessed: September 12, 2023.

"Johnson County War" https://www.wyominghistoryday.org/theme-topics/johnson-county-war Accessed: September 12, 2023.

"Butch Cassidy in Wyoming" https://www.wyohistory.org/encyclopedia/butch-cassidy-wyoming Accessed: September 13, 2023.

"Tom Horn – Wyoming Killer for Hire" https://www.legendsofamerica.com/we-tomhorn/ Accessed: September 13, 2023.

"Harry Longabaugh, aka 'Sundance Kid' – Member of the Wild Bunch" https://www.legendsofamerica.com/sundance-kid/ Accessed: September 13, 2023.

"Cattle Kate – Mystery of a Lynching" https://www.legendsofamerica.com/we-cattlekate/ Accessed: September 13, 2023.

Chapter 6

"Women's Suffrage and Women's Rights" https://www.wyohistory.org/encyclopedia/topics/womens-suffrage-and-womens-rights Accessed: September 14, 2023.

"Woman Suffrage" https://education.nationalgeographic.org/resource/woman-suffrage/ Accessed: September 14, 2023.

Larson, T.A., 1965. "Woman Suffrage in Wyoming." *The Pacific Northwest Quarterly* (56:2), pp 57-66.

"Esther Hobart Morris – Justice of the Peace and Icon of Women's Rights" https://www.wyohistory.org/encyclopedia/esther-hobart-morris-justice-peace-and-icon-womens-rights Accessed: September 15, 2023.

"Amalia Post- Defender of Women's Rights" https://www.wyohistory.org/encyclopedia/amalia-post-defender-womens-rights Accessed: September 15, 2023.

"To 'Hold a More Brilliant Torch:' Suffragist and Orator Theresa Jenkins" https://www.wyohistory.org/encyclopedia/hold-more-brilliant-torch-suffragist-and-orator-theresa-jenkins Accessed: September 15, 2023.

Grace Raymond Hebard: Shaping Wyoming's Past https://www.wyohistory.org/encyclopedia/grace-raymond-hebard-shaping-wyomings-past Accessed: November 9, 2023.

Mary Godat Bellamy, Wyoming's First Woman Legislator https://www.wyohistory.org/encyclopedia/mary-godat-bellamy Accessed: November 9, 2023.

Chapter 7

"Wyoming Becomes a State: The Constitutional Convention and Statehood Debates of 1889 and 1890 and Their Aftermath" https://www.wyohistory.org/encyclopedia/wyoming-statehood Accessed: September 16, 2023.

"Wyoming becomes 44th state July 10, 1890" https://www.politico.com/story/2007/07/wyoming-becomes-44th-state-july-10-1890-004845 Accessed: September 17, 2023.

Chapter 8

"The Oil Business in Wyoming" https://www.wyohistory.org/encyclopedia/oil-business-wyoming Accessed: September 20, 2023.

"First Wyoming Oil Wells" https://aoghs.org/petroleum-pioneers/first-wyoming-oil-well/ Accessed: September 20, 2023.

"Boom and Bust in the Salt Creek Oil Field" https://www.wyohistory.org/education/toolkit/boom-and-bust-salt-creek-oil-field#:~:text=In%201923%2C%20the%20year%20of,of%20the%20ground%20was%20falling. Accessed: September 20, 2023.

"Wyoming's Energy Economy in Transition" https://www.resources.org/resources-radio/wyomings-energy-economy-in-transition-with-robert-godby/ Accessed: September 20, 2023.

"Oil to Market: A History of Pipelines in Wyoming" https://www.wyohistory.org/encyclopedia/oil-market-history-pipelines-wyoming Accessed: September 20, 2023.

"The Jonah Field and Pinedale Anticline: A natural-gas success story" https://www.wyohistory.org/encyclopedia/jonah-field-and-pinedale-anticline-natural-gas-success-story Accessed: September 20, 2023.

"The Coal Business in Wyoming" https://www.wyohistory.org/encyclopedia/coal-business-wyoming Accessed: September 20, 2023.

Chapter 9

"Economic diversification: an old optic that deserves new attention" https://wyofile.com/economic-diversification-an-old-topic-that-deserves-new-attention/ Accessed: September 22, 2023.

"Wyoming in the 20th Century" https://www.britannica.com/place/Wyoming-state/Wyoming-in-the-20th-century Accessed: September 22, 2023.

Knoblach, Frieda, 2001. "Creating the Cowboy State: Culture and Underdevelopment in Wyoming Since 1867." *Western Historical Quarterly* (32:2) pp. 201-221.

"Wyoming Government and Society" https://www.britannica.com/place/Wyoming-state/Government-and-society Accessed: September 22, 2023.

Chapter 10

"Wyoming" https://www.nps.gov/state/wy/index.htm Accessed: September 23, 2023.

"Wyoming National Parks, National Monuments and National Recreation Areas" https://www.americansouthwest.net/wyoming/national-parks.html Accessed: September 23, 2023.

Printed in the USA
CPSIA information can be obtained
at www.ICGtesting.com
LVHW012341060124
768131LV00007B/277